MYTH

OR

LEGEND?

G. E. DANIEL   J. M. WHITE

D. L. PAGE   E. R. LEACH

R. F. TREHARNE   T. C. LETHBRIDGE

SIR L. WOOLLEY   S. PIGGOTT

C. T. SELTMAN   J. S. P. BRADFORD

S. P. Ó RÍORDÁIN   H. J. ROSE

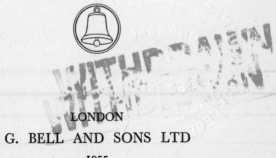

LONDON

G. BELL AND SONS LTD

1955

19008

First published February 1955
Reprinted June 1955

Printed in Great Britain by
NEILL & CO. LTD., EDINBURGH

Preface

IN the autumn of 1952 Donald Boyd, Chief Assistant in the Talks Department of the B.B.C., had the idea of a series of talks in which various speakers were to examine well-known stories like that of the Golden Bough (which was used by Sir James Frazer as the title of his great anthropological work), or Minos and the Minotaur, or King Arthur, and were to decide, in the light of modern historical and archæological knowledge, whether there was any truth in them. The series was devised and produced by Michael Stephens of the B.B.C. Talks staff, and I was very happy to be associated with him in the preliminary discussions about the stories and places that might be included. The first series of six talks was given in the spring of 1953; a further series of six was given in the winter of 1953-4. Some of these have already been printed in *The Listener*. They are now all printed here in this book. None has been re-written for publication; they are, essentially, what they were meant to be, the scripts of talks, and will, I hope, meet the requirements of many who wrote asking for one or other—or all—of the talks to be issued in permanent form.

The theme of the twelve talks is the theme set out by Donald Boyd, and set out also in *The Radio Times* when the series began, in these words

'It makes a good story but—is it true? For anyone who wants a good story *and* an answer to that tiresome little question which threatens to spoil the whole effect . . . this . . . is exactly the right prescription. . . . The difference between myth and legend, between invention and fancy on one hand and some kind of history on the other, is the theme of this new series of talks.'

I have tried myself in my talk on *Lyonesse*, which introduced the series, to explain the difference between myth and legend, as these terms are used by historians, archæologists and students of folk-tale. The myth is an invented story, the legend, on the other hand, has a basis of history, however confused and obscured by later additions. The writers and speakers of these talks were throughout asking themselves these questions about the place or subject given to them as a topic: Is it true? Is it false? in a word, Myth or Legend?

GLYN E. DANIEL

Cambridge, 1954

Contents

List of Plates

List of Figures

Acknowledgments

Permission has been given for the inclusion of certain copyright material, and grateful acknowledgment is made to:—

The contributors for many pictures and much help in a variety of ways.

The Controller of H.M. Stationery Office and the Air Ministry for Plate 3.

The Archæological Expedition of the University of Cincinnati and C. W. Blegen, editor of *Troy* Volume III, for Plates 4 and 5, and Miss Marion Rawson for providing the original photographs.

The Cambridge University Press for Plate 8.

The Oxford University Press for Plate 9.

Messrs. Dundalgan Press (W. Tempest) Ltd., Dundalk, for Plate 14 and fig. iii.

London Calling of Broadcasting House, London, for Plate 16.

The Curator of the Royal Institution of Cornwall at Truro for Plate 17.

The Ministry of Works for Plate 18.

The Italian State Tourist Department in London for Plate 19.

I

Lyonesse and the Lost Lands of England

G. E. DANIEL

THE lost land of Lyonesse—it is a romantic alliterative phrase—and the story of Lyonesse is also a romantic one.

> A land of matchless grace was Lyonesse
> Glorious with rolling hills, rejoicing streams
> Hoar monuments upreared when Time was young
> Wide plains of forest, slopes of golden corn,
> And stately castles crowning granite peaks.

So says the poet; but Lyonesse is no poetic fancy. The story of Lyonesse is widely believed by many in Cornwall and in south-west Britain generally. The story briefly is this. Once upon a time there was a land between Cornwall and the Isles of Scilly which lie about thirty-five miles away. This land was called Lyonesse; or in Cornish Lethowstow. It was extremely rich; it had rich and prosperous towns and a hundred and forty churches. Camden in the sixteenth century said that Land's End once undoubtedly stretched far to the west, and that there had been to the west a watchtower with lights to direct mariners. Sir Richard Carew, a contemporary of Camden's and a friend of Sir Walter Raleigh—and Gibson who edited Camden's

Britannia in the late seventeenth century—speak of the rocks called the Seven Stones, seven miles west of Land's End, and how many people thought they were the remains of a great city. Fishermen were said to have dragged up windows and similar pieces of buildings from the remains of this city—the City of Lions it was called. The Seven Sisters are still sometimes called 'The Town'.

What was the fate of this rich and fertile country of Lyonesse? The traditions vary in detail but substantially the story they tell is the same. The land of Lyonesse was overwhelmed by the sea, and the sole survivor was a man called Trevilian who leapt on a swift horse and fled to the mainland. And that is why, say the tales, the Trevilians bear as arms a horse issuing out of the sea.

Sir Thomas Malory talks of Surluse as part of the kingdom of Lyonesse where Sir Galahad was ruler under King Arthur. Spenser in *The Faerie Queene* makes Tristram be born in Lyonesse:

> Out of the countrie, wherein I was bred,
> The which the fertile *Lionesse* is hight . . .

And so does Milton:

> Fairy Damsels met in Forest wide
> By Knights of *Logres*, or of *Lyones* . . .

And Tennyson describes the end of Arthur in Lyonesse:

> So all day long the noise of battle roll'd
> Among the mountains by the winter sea;
> Until King Arthur's Table, man by man,
> Had fall'n in Lyonesse about their lord,
> King Arthur . . .

and he describes the 'sweet land of Lyonesse':

> A land of old upheaven from the abyss
> By fire, to sink into the abyss again;
> Where fragments of forgotten peoples dwelt,
> And the long mountains ended in a coast
> Of ever-shifting sand, and far away
> The phantom circle of a moaning sea.

A story much the same as this tale of Lyonesse is told of areas on the west coast of Wales. Here Lyonesse is replaced by Cantre'r Gwaelod, the Lowland Cantref, or, if we can translate the Welsh freely into a modern idiom, the parishes that have been submerged. And the stories of Cantre'r Gwaelod are all essentially the same; they describe a ruler of a Cantref in Cardiganshire—a man who ruled over what is now submerged land in Cardigan Bay from St. David's Head to Borth near Aberystwyth. Cantre'r Gwaelod, like Lyonesse, was supposed to be rich and prosperous, its splendour was proverbial, we hear of the richness and trade of its sixteen towns. Then came disaster. It was inundated by the sea. The Welsh traditions refer specifically to the king's drunken steward who opened the flood gates and let in the sea. And this Welsh tale of Cantre'r Gwaelod is burlesqued, by the way, in Thomas Love Peacock's novel *The Misfortunes of Elphin*.

Farther north in Wales, in Caernarvonshire, between Conway and Penmon, we again meet the same story. This time it refers to what are now called the Lafan Sands; it was formerly known as Tyno Helig. There is the same sudden advance of the sea, but this time the inundation is the spectacular fulfilment of a long promised divine vengeance brought down on Helig, the ruler of the kingdom—vengeance on his own wickedness and that of his forbears. Helig and his family,

MYTH OR LEGEND?

by the way, are reported to have escaped, and ever after lived godly lives.

And yet again the same tale occurs in Brittany; here Lyonesse and the lowland Cantref become Ker-Is. Ker, by the way, is the same as the Welsh word Caer which appears in Caernarvon and Caermarthen and the Cornish Car—it means town or fort or city, and Ker-Is merely means the lowland city, or, in a word, the submerged city. Ker-Is, in Breton folklore, was a city submerged due to the wickedness of its inhabitants and the negligence of those who held the keys of the sea fortifications. Ker-Is is located in the Bay of Douarne-nez in that part of western Brittany still called Cor-nouailles or Cornwall, but the story is a well-established folk-tale in western Brittany generally.

They are all good stories, in a sense they are all the same story, but here is our problem: Are they imagina-tion, or have they any basis, however slight, in fact? Are they, to put a point on it, myths or legends? And, by the way, I am using these two words in an exact and differentiated sense. In an ordinary way of speaking we talk of myths and legends as though the words were interchangeable. But students of folk-tales and tradi-tions do distinguish between myth and legend: they say that myth is an invented story—invented perhaps to explain some extraordinary natural event like an earthquake, or something far less catastrophic like the daily rising and setting of the sun, or a human event like dreams—which after all are very puzzling to primitive peoples; and they say that legend, on the other hand, is not an invented story—it is a form of history. It may have all sorts of odd things added to it—there may be plenty of inventions and myths wrapped round the legend, but basically the legend has a kernel of truth, however distorted. And—this is an important point—often we do not realise that a folk-tale is a legend, or could be a legend, until historical and archæological research reveals the historical fact enshrined in it.

And now to get back to our lost lands. Are these stories of lost lands—and particularly the story of Lyonesse—invented stories, or genuine historical memories—myths or legends? Now let me say at once there is no agreement on the answer to this question. Many people say they are myths, and it is very easy to see how these myths could arise. There are in Cardigan Bay extensive areas of shoal water, and there are two submerged causeways running for several miles out to sea; they are called Sarn y Bwlch and Sarn Cynvelyn. Geologists tell us that these causeways are entirely of natural origin, but they could have given rise to the story of the lowland Cantref. From high land they can easily be seen, and could have been turned into the dykes of the folk-tales. There is shoal water too between the Isles of Scilly; sometimes at neap-tide it is possible to walk from one island to another. Then the finding at low tide of the remains of submerged forests in Cardigan Bay and in Mount's Bay might have given rise to myths of inundated lands.

Those who argue that these stories are myths point out—and it is quite true—that traditions of lands and cities overwhelmed by the sea are very common in western Europe. All along the coasts of France and Germany one can find these stories. Are they then universal stories, have they something in common with the Christian inheritance—the memory of the Deluge for example? Are the stories of Lyonesse and Ker-Is no more than universal deluge stories localised

in Brittany, Cornwall and Wales: localised because of
the appearance of obvious things like the causeways in
Cardigan Bay or the submerged forests in Mount's Bay?
That is what some people say; and in discussing
Lyonesse, for example, they point to the fact that the
story does not appear until after the Norman Conquest.
But I am not sure that this argument is a very good one;
we have very few written traditions from pre-Norman
days, and because a tradition was not recorded for
hundreds of years we cannot argue that it was not orally
transmitted—or, I grant you, for that matter, that it
was.   I am only trying to say that, because the tradition
of Lyonesse cannot be dated back in written form before
the twelfth century, we are not entitled to argue that it
was a myth invented in the twelfth century.   It may
still be a myth, but it may on the other hand be a
legend.

I rather think it is a legend; I am on the side of those
who think these stories have historical value—some
historical value, and I say *some* deliberately.   I do not
believe there is any justification for the rich cities; and,
of course, the wicked stewards and all the rest of it, and
even perhaps King Arthur himself, are just embellish-
ments in an age of romance and courtly tales.   I think
it is likely that these tales are legends enshrining an
historical or, if you like, a prehistorical fact—the
memory of a time when the land in parts of Brittany,
Cornwall and west Wales was more extensive than it is
at present.   You may say that this is just my personal
opinion; that may be so, but it is the opinion of many
other archæologists and historians who have studied
this problem.   And what is not a matter of personal
opinion is the fact that the land in Wales, south-west
Britain and Brittany did once stand further out than at

Photo Gibson

2. Old Field Walls on the flats between the Isles of Scilly

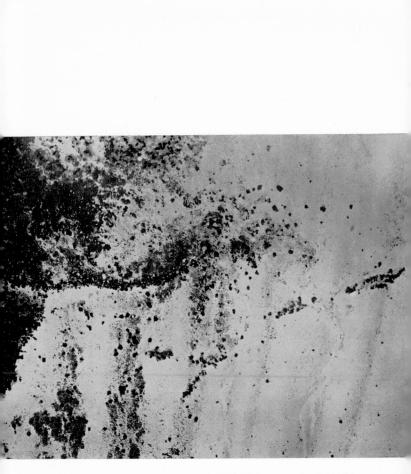

3. Aerial photograph of Old Field Walls between the Scilly Isles

present. Nowhere is this evidence of submergence more dramatic and convincing than in the Isles of Scilly and Mount's Bay—just those areas where Lyonesse was supposed to have been (Plates 2 and 3).

On the flats between the small Isles of Scilly are field walls—walls now under the sea—which divided the land before it was submerged. Recently an Early Iron Age house was excavated at St. Martin's in the Scillies; it was on the beach below high-water mark. In 1948, on the shores of the same island, part of a circular hut was found—it dated from the Roman period; there was pottery of the third and fourth centuries A.D., and the floor of this hut is covered by normal high tides. At Old Man—another island in the Scillies, or rather two islands (it is a small island recently cut into two—the most recent example of coastal erosion)—at Old Man was found, also below normal high-water mark, a burial cist or stone grave containing two Roman bronze brooches of the mid-first century A.D. All this, and much more evidence which geologists, pollen analysts, geographers and archæologists have been painstakingly collecting for years—evidence which cannot be set aside—show that as late as Roman times the sea between the Isles of Scilly was dry land; in fact that there was one Isle of Scilly, not an archipelago of isles and islets as at present. This is quite interesting in one way—I mean that Scilly may have been a single island as late as the Roman period—because a Roman writer tells us that in A.D. 387 a heretic was banished to Sylina Insula, the *island* of Scilly.

I have mentioned the submerged forests in Mount's Bay. Now we know also, through the work of petrologists and archæologists, that there is actually an axe

B

factory, dating from, say, 1800 to 1500 B.C., somewhere in Mount's Bay under the sea. We have clear proof of submergence in south-west Britain—and submergence well within historical times—in Roman times in the Isles of Scilly. The submergence of the Scillies is a historical event which could have lived in memory and become enshrined in the much elaborated tale of Lyonesse. I believe it did. It is for you to decide in the light of the arguments I have mentioned. Do not be put off by those who insist that all traditions must be unhistoric; I know that a lot of them are. But to say that Lyonesse is a historical tradition, or may well be a historical tradition, is not to argue that all traditions are historical and that there are no myths. Of course there are myths; I suspect that Lyonesse and the other lost lands of western Britain is not one of them. And do not be put off by people who say that traditions cannot be transmitted orally for hundreds of years; that is an ignorant assumption by those who have not studied the oral transmission of tales. The best example that comes to my mind is from India. The Rig Vedas first written down in the eighteenth century A.D. preserve a most accurate picture of the cities which the Aryan invaders met in India when they invaded it in, let us say, the eighteenth century B.C. And nobody believed it until excavation in the last thirty years revealed these cities.

But we are wandering from Lyonesse. There is one final question you may ask. If Lyonesse, Cantre'r Gwaelod, and Ker-Is are then folk-tales with a kernel of truth in them, a memory of former lands under the sea, what of other similar folk-tales that abound? What about St. Brandon's Isles, the Isle of Brazil, the Green Island, marked on charts until the middle of the nineteenth century? What about Atlantis, the Isles of the Bless'd, and the Flood itself? And what about King Arthur, whom some of the traditions associate with Lyonesse? Are these also legends, or are they myths? But these are questions that will be answered in other chapters in this book.

SUGGESTIONS FOR FURTHER READING

A classic memoir on submergence and submerged lands was Clement Reid's *Submerged Forests*, published in 1913 in the Cambridge Manuals of Science and Literature. In the first number of the quarterly journal *Antiquity*, the editor, Dr. O. G. S. Crawford, wrote an article called 'Lyonesse' (*Antiquity*, 1927, p. 5 ff.) with photographs of the features, possibly submerged walls, between the islands. H. O'Neil Hencken's *Archæology of Cornwall and Scilly* (1932) gives a general account of the problem of Lyonesse and the isles of Scilly. Mrs. Rachel Bromwich's article 'Cantre'r Gwaelod and Ker-Is' in *The Early Cultures of North-West Europe* (H. M. Chadwick Memorial Studies, ed. Fox and Dickins, Cambridge, 1950) p. 217 ff. gives an up-to-date account of the Celtic folklore and literature about submerged lands.

II

The City of Troy

DENYS PAGE

AMONG the greatest works in European literature is the oldest of them all, the *Iliad*; an epic poem, over 15,000 lines, on the subject of Troy. The Greeks themselves could only guess when it was written and who wrote it. Their historical memory went back as far as the eighth century B.C., but no further. Behind that time there lay a great darkness of about four hundred years; and from that darkness there came no clear light, except what might be found in the *Iliad*; which described, in considerable detail, life as it had been lived, not during the Dark Ages, but before they ever began. It was remarkable that this portrait of the past should have survived so long; still more remarkable that it should reveal a state of civilisation much more advanced than anything that followed it for five or six hundred years; and most remarkable of all that the poem itself should be of a quality never surpassed in the history of ancient literature.

The *Iliad* tells the story of an episode in the siege of Troy, a fortress located in the extreme north-west corner of Asia Minor, overlooking, from the south, the strait of the Dardanelles. The episode is confined to a few days in the tenth year of the war; but the background of the story is clear enough: Paris, a son of

King Priam of Troy, visited the palace of Menelaus, King of Sparta, in southern Greece. There he fell captive to the beauty of Helen, the wife of Menelaus; and secretly, not without packing a great quantity of Helen's clothes and jewellery, the pair departed by night for Troy. But Menelaus' brother, Agamemnon, was King of all Kings in Greece; and, to avenge this insult to his family, he commanded his barons to assemble at the harbour of Aulis; and from Aulis a great fleet sailed for Troy. There was fighting at the walls of Troy for ten years. When at last the city was taken, the Greeks returned home; and soon, for whatever reason, there fell over Greece that darkness without a history for four hundred years.

This story of the love of Paris and Helen, of the ten years' siege of Troy, of its capture and destruction, remained for the rest of time the most famous of ancient stories. And the *Iliad* remained the most famous of all poems; no work, in prose or poetry, was ever thought to surpass it. It was a common feat, in an age before the memory was ruined by reading, to know the whole of it by heart. And there was never any suggestion that the story might not be true. The detail, of course, was criticised: Thucydides, the greatest of ancient historians, thought that much of it was embroidered and exaggerated; but for him, as for all reasonable men at all times, the substance of the tale was history, not myth. Nor was there any serious doubt about the date of these events: the Trojan War, it was generally agreed, began soon after the year 1200 B.C.

The *Iliad*, then, embodied and preserved the past splendours of the nation; it remained the most valuable heirloom of Greece, until darkness fell a second time upon European humanity, not to be broken until the dawn of the Italian renaissance.

The scene shifts to Germany, to Fuerstenberg, a small town fifty miles north of Berlin. There, in the year 1836, an unlikely boy, aged fourteen, was serving (according to his own account) 'herrings and potato-whisky' across the counter in a grocer's shop. Heinrich Schliemann had seen better days. He was the son of a Protestant clergyman; and he had known the tale of Troy, from his father, since childhood. At the age of seven, he says, 'with great grief I heard from him that Troy had been so completely destroyed that it had disappeared without leaving any traces of its existence'. Laughed at by his little world, but fortified by the faith and devotion of a good woman, also aged seven, he decided then and there that he had a single ambition in life—to discover Troy.

But the family fell into hard times, and there was Heinrich, from the age of fourteen to nineteen, serving in the grocer's shop from five in the morning till eleven at night. There was no chance of learning Greek: the vision of Troy was faded; faith needed nourishment. So one day, when Hermann Niederhoeffer, a miller by trade, was drunk as usual, Providence guided him to that source of potato-whisky, and propped him against the counter, thickly declaiming verses from the *Iliad*, remembered from a happier past. Heinrich could not understand a word; but the cup of faith was replenished within him. 'Three times over did I get him to repeat to me those divine verses, rewarding his trouble with three glasses of whisky, which I bought with the few pence that made up my whole fortune. From that moment I never ceased to pray God that by His grace I might yet have the happiness of learning Greek.'

But first a fortune must be made, surely in a wider
world than Fuerstenberg. Oppressed by illness and
poverty, but not despair, Schliemann went to Hamburg,
where he sold his only coat to buy a blanket, and, as a
cabin-boy, joined the brig *Dorothea*. It was not the
straightest path to his goal; for he was not far out of
harbour on his first voyage when down went the brig.
The cabin-boy narrowly escaped to the coast of Holland;
and there, slowly enough, his fortune took a better
turn. He found employment in Amsterdam at £32 a
year, and had leisure to learn languages: first, English,
mastered in six months by an unusual method: he
learned by heart the whole of *Ivanhoe* and *The Vicar of
Wakefield*, and recited these to his astonished tutor.
Then French and Russian on the same principles.
The reward of his industry was a post in Moscow as
agent for his company; and there he built up a very
large business in the import trade. By the age of
thirty-two he was a rich man: the vision of Troy
appeared in brighter colours; and there was time to
learn Greek. First, modern Greek, mastered in six
weeks; and, in the next six months, enough ancient
Greek to read the *Iliad* and *Odyssey* 'with the most
lively enthusiasm'.

When he was forty-one years old, Schliemann
decided that his wealth was now sufficient for its sole
purpose—the discovery and excavation of Troy. He
sold his business, and invested the proceeds to return
an annual income of £10,000. He travelled round
the world; studied archæology in Paris; and in 1868
landed on the south coast of the Dardanelles. There,
in the Trojan plain, he saw a hill, Hissarlik, standing
up to about 160 feet above sea-level; he felt convinced
that it was not what it appeared, a hill; it was the city

of Troy, barely hidden by a cover of earth. The learned world was vastly amused when, in the fullness of time, he began to dig.

Schliemann was looking for a city of Troy: he found nine cities of Troy, layer upon layer, from the hill-top to bedrock. The faith of nearly forty years was surely confirmed when, far down, just above the oldest settlement, the outlines of a fortress worthy of the *Iliad* began to appear. Here, laid bare by spade and pick-axe, arose a small but immensely strong citadel, about 360 yards in circuit, enclosed by a massive wall roughly circular in plan, with towers projecting at intervals, and two large gateways. You may see the wall best near the south-east gate: three feet of stone foundation, supporting a wall of mud-brick faced with stone, twelve feet thick, and still ten feet high in places. Inside the fortress one house at least was worthy of King Priam; for its main room is sixty feet long, and half as broad. The wealth and culture of this, the second city of Troy, was illustrated by a wonderful discovery: Schliemann himself had the good fortune to find, abandoned on the wall 4,000 years ago, a hoard of treasures in gold, silver and bronze. There is something romantic in the list of articles, especially item 22, '56 gold earrings', and item 23, '8,700 gold rings'. And if Troy was captured by the army of Agamemnon, this surely was the city; for beyond all question it was destroyed by fire—there are heaps of corn, burnt to charcoal; masses of molten bronze; bones and oyster-shell incinerated; and the walls themselves, made of unbaked mud, are partly baked into brickwork by enormous heat.

And yet this was not, as Schliemann died believing, the Troy of the *Iliad*. Soon after his death, one of the most eminent archæologists of his time, Wilhelm

Doerpfeld, made still greater discoveries on the hill of Hissarlik, bringing to light the walls of another and later city of Troy: and the pottery and other objects found there proved that it is *this* city which coincides in date with the Troy of Priam's fathers. This is a much larger fortress with a circuit of about 600 yards, enclosed by walls of great beauty and strength. The quality of the stonework varies from one point to another: at its best, it is ashlar masonry of uncommon craftsmanship—limestone blocks, about five feet long, one foot high and deep, so shaped and so laid that the joins are sometimes hardly visible to the eye. The wall is about fifteen feet thick, and was originally about thirty feet high; long ranges of it now stand exposed, in perfect preservation, up to eighteen feet in height (Plates 4 and 5, facing p. 32).

Huge towers project from it at intervals; three massive gateways may still be seen. Inside the walls, you have to imagine a hill, with houses built on terraces in a series of concentric circles from the summit to the base; with paved streets radiating upwards from the wall, piercing the terraces at right-angles, and converging at the top of the hill, like the spokes of a wheel.

This, the sixth city, collapsed in an earthquake about 1300 B.C., but was soon rebuilt; and the great American archæologist, Carl Blegen, who re-excavated Troy between 1932 and 1938, has shown that it is this, the rebuilt fortress (which we call Troy No. Seven), which was inhabited at the date of the Ten Years' War.

It is at this point that myth and legend make perfect harmony: for the myth told us of a great siege and great sack of Troy about 1200 B.C.; and history, in huge walls, and skeletons of men transfixed by the spear 3,000 years ago, and relics of a citadel in flames, shows us—not merely tells us—that this massive stronghold was captured and burned about that very date, and was (for the first time in 2,000 years) abandoned by civilised men. We do not know that its king was called Priam or its hero Hector; or whether Helen was the cause of war and, if so, how many ships her beauty launched. The poets of the *Iliad* remembered much, but they also imagined much; for more than one reason it is vain to dig for relics of the Wooden Horse. Archæology has shown that the great and wealthy kingdom of Agamemnon is not myth but history; and it teaches the same lesson in the tale of Troy. We can distinguish, at least in part, between the fabric and the embroidery; and the fabric stands on the plain of Troy, massive walls and towers translating fable into history.

SUGGESTIONS FOR FURTHER READING

The standard work is *Troy*, edited by C. W. Blegen (Princeton University Press, Vol. I, 1950, Vol. II, 1951, Vol. III, 1953); no other book is really up to date. H. Schliemann's own publications are very good reading, though outmoded archæologically. They are: *Troy and its Remains* (1875), *Ilios, the City and Country of the Trojans* (1880), *Troja* (1884).

Emil Ludwig's excellent life of Schliemann (*Schliemann of Troy*, 1931) makes very enjoyable reading. Of all books in English about the *Iliad* the most interesting is Gilbert Murray's *Rise of the Greek Epic* (4th ed. 1934).

III

Glastonbury
and the Holy Grail

R. F. TREHARNE

GLASTONBURY TOR was designed by nature to attract men, history and legend. Has any place in Britain a longer history of unbroken human life, or a more involved tangle of gossamer fancy and hard fact for the story of its past? It is the fairy isle of Avalon, where Arthur lies waiting his call to rescue the world once more from heathen savagery and evil men. A mile away is Pomparlès, the 'Bridge Perilous' over the little River Brue, where he cast Excalibur into the water. Barely a dozen miles off stands Cadbury Castle, the 'many-towered Camelot' of the legend. (The Tor is shown in Plate 6, pp. 32–3.)

Still more, it was to Glastonbury, first of all places in Britain, that our Christian faith came. When the Apostle Philip, the companion of Jesus, had converted Gaul, he sent a great company of his followers, led by Joseph of Arimathea, to evangelise Britain in the year 63. Joseph brought with him the Holy Grail, the sacred chalice of the Last Supper, in which he had collected Christ's blood at the Crucifixion. Approaching Glastonbury after many strange adventures, the disciples rested awhile on the little rise half a mile south-west of the Tor. When Joseph stopped to pray at the foot of the Tor, his staff took root and budded, a miraculous sign that he had reached his journey's end. The local king, Arviragus, though he rejected Joseph's gospel, gave him the firm land around the Tor for his settlement. 'Ynys Vitrin' the British called it —'the isle of woad'. Here Joseph built the first Christian church in Britain, and here he buried the Grail. His rooted staff became the Glastonbury Thorn, flowering every Christmas to honour Christ's birth, and the little hill where they had rested was called Wearyall Hill. The Grail became the object of the mystic quest of King Arthur's knights, thus linking together the two otherwise separate legends. Finally, in 1191, the monks of Glastonbury discovered the bodies of King Arthur and Queen Guinevere, lying buried within their walls, with a leaden cross inscribed: 'Here lies buried the renowned King Arthur, with Guinevere his second wife, in the Isle of Avalon.' Such is the essence of the Glastonbury story: how much of it is fable, how much history?

About the year 1125 a great monastic chronicler, William of Malmesbury, visited Glastonbury Abbey, and wrote a book *On the Antiquity of the Church of Glastonbury*, recording what the monks told him about their famous house. Successive Glastonbury writers frequently re-edited this book, so that, in its surviving form, it tells what men believed about one hundred and twenty years later, and not what William had originally written. But fortunately about 1140, William had copied his original account of Glastonbury's history into a bigger book, *The Deeds of the Kings of Britain*, and by comparing these two books we can see what William heard in 1125, and what the tradition was one hundred and twenty years later.

William's account of Glastonbury's history is detailed, careful and critical: he did not believe all he was told. He saw the primitive little church of wattles and clay, the holy of holies of Glastonbury, which they told him was the first Christian church built in Britain. He carefully refused to commit himself to the story that St. Philip's disciples had built it in the year 63. If St. Philip really did evangelise Gaul, he commented, then he might well have sent missionaries into Britain. William preferred the alternative story that the wattle church was built in the year 166, by emissaries of the Pope, sent at the request of Lucius, King of Britain. This was a genuine misunderstanding: there was no king of Roman Britain in A.D. 166, and Lucius ruled, not in Britain, but at Birtha in Mesopotamia. The rest of William's story is of the ever-growing fame and holiness of the little church, a centre of pilgrimage and the home of saints innumerable. St. Patrick came from Ireland in 432 and organised the colony of scattered hermits at Glastonbury into a monastery, which he ruled as abbot for thirty years. St. Bridget of Ireland, St. Gildas the historian, and St. David of Wales all came to live there, and St. Paulinus, the first Archbishop of York, piously covered the little church with timber and lead, to protect it from the weather. Such was the fame of this ancient shrine that when, in 658, it fell into English hands, the English, now themselves Christian, outdid the British in lavishing gifts upon it.

But in all this, although William is profoundly impressed by the antiquity of Glastonbury, there is no mention of Joseph of Arimathea, the Holy Grail, or

King Arthur. Yet William knew of Arthur, for elsewhere he wrote: 'This is that Arthur concerning whom
the idle tales of the Britons rave wildly even to-day.'
The historic Arthur he praises, though he does not
link him with Glastonbury. He will have none of the
Arthur of romance. Hitherto the story of Arthur had
been exclusively Celtic; but about the year 1135 that
amazing romancer, Geoffrey of Monmouth, published
his fabulous *History of the Kings of Britain*, translated, he
said, from an old Welsh book. To an astonished and
delighted world Geoffrey gave the core of the Arthurian
legend, essentially Celtic and more than half pagan
myth, only superficially touched with French and
Christian chivalry. Arthur was here portrayed as the
heroic British warrior-king, not as the idealised medieval
knight of the Anglo-French poets, of Sir Thomas
Malory and of Tennyson. Of Joseph of Arimathea
and the Holy Grail, Geoffrey says nothing. He tells
that Arthur, mortally wounded in battle at the River
Camlan, 'was carried thence to Avalon for the healing
of his wounds', but Geoffrey never identifies Avalon
with Glastonbury. His Insula Avallonis 'Ynys Afalon',
'the isle of apples', is a magic isle of healing and plenty,
far in the western ocean, but really not of this world at
all. It is the Celtic counterpart of the Greek Hesperides,
the islands of the golden apples.

Despite scornful denunciations from exasperated
historians, Geoffrey became a best-seller almost over-
night. No twelfth-century writer was more widely
read, copied and plagiarised. In the next seventy years
legends from all over Europe had been grafted on to
Geoffrey's stock, and the half-pagan Celtic story had
been Europeanised and Christianised by adding the
mystic *motif* of the Holy Grail. Arthur became the

Princeton U.P.

4. Troy VI: East Wall and Tower VI H, as excavated by Carl W. Blegen
in 1938, seen from the south

Princeton U.P.

5. Troy VI: East Wall and north side of Tower VI H, seen from the
north-east. Both pictures by courtesy of the University of Cincinatti
Archæological Department

7. Glastonbury Lady Chapel, built on the site of the old wattle church after the fire of 1184

Photo C.U.P.

8. St Joseph of Arimathea, bearing the two cruets,
from the east window of Langport Church

knightly king, with his lovely queen, Guinevere, his Round Table of noble knights, and all the panoply of chivalry and magic that a romantic age could devise. Soon men attempted to locate the legends, and in 1194, in recounting the discovery of the bodies of Arthur and Guinevere, Gerald of Wales first identified Avalon with Glastonbury. How had this become possible?

On May 25th, 1186, the whole abbey, including the wattle church, was destroyed by fire. The abbot and monks launched a national appeal, under royal patronage, for funds to rebuild the abbey on a scale commensurate with its fame, and in two years received money enough to build the beautiful new Lady Chapel on the site of the wattle church (Plate 7). The appeal then wilted, with the vast new church barely begun. To meet this desperate crisis, Arthur and Guinevere had to be discovered, since an age which read far more of Arthur and his knights than of the whole calendar of saints, would subscribe with enthusiasm for a church worthy of this popular discovery. Arthur and Joseph of Arimathea, so recently linked together by the myth of the Grail, were now firmly grafted on to the stock of the Glastonbury tradition, to flourish there ever since.

The new legend swiftly submerged the older tradition, though so little of it was true. The Arthur of the romances, with Queen Guinevere and the Knights of the Round Table, are nothing more than imaginary figures in the greatest of all romances. A real Arthur, indeed, there was, dimly discerned by historians, winning imperishable fame by his gloriously successful resistance to the invading Saxons about the end of the fifth century. No king of Britain, or of any other realm, Arthur was simply a country gentleman who became a great cavalry general and won glory as the

c

saviour of his people in their hour of need.   Nothing
in history links him with Glastonbury, though of
course we cannot assert that he never visited so sacred
a shrine.   Who knows where he lies?   'A grave there
is for Mark, a grave for Gwythur, a Grave for Gwgawn
of the Red Sword: a marvel till the day of judgment
the grave of Arthur', said the Welsh poet.   We need
not doubt that when Gerald of Wales visited Glastonbury, he saw the two bodies which he says had been
found a year or two earlier.   Perhaps the monks had
unearthed a genuine Celtic burial;   perhaps some
genius with a flair for advertisement had simply trans-
planted into the monastery grounds the skeletons of
some nameless Celtic chief and his wife, buried a
thousand years earlier in a dug-out canoe near the
pre-historic lake-village below the Tor.   But whoever
they were, they were not Arthur and Guinevere of the
romances, for these were beings incorporeal, whose
feet had never trod this heavy earth of ours.   Nor was
it the Arthur of history whose skeleton Gerald saw,
for he would have had Christian burial.

And what of the Grail?   That, too, is mingled myth
and legend.   To be fair, the monks of Glastonbury
never claimed to have it.   The Church mistrusted the
story of the Grail, and never officially recognised it.
At Glastonbury the monks said that St. Joseph had
brought, not the Grail, but two glass cruets containing
the blood and the sweat of Christ, and these were
buried with Joseph, not mysteriously hidden.   They
figure clearly in the late medieval glass of the east
window of Langport Church nearby (Plate 8).   But
popular fancy insisted on the Grail, and popular fancy
had its way.

As for Joseph, we must not assert that it is impossible

that he should have come to Glastonbury. We do not know what became of him after the Resurrection, and, once Rome had conquered Britain, a rich Jewish merchant could have travelled more easily in the next thirty years from Palestine to Glastonbury than at any time in the Middle Ages. Beyond this we cannot go. The story is an extremely late tradition, bearing every mark of invention, and no historian would assert its probability. Chalice Well must go with the Grail, and Wearyall Hill is clearly a too ingenious attempt to explain 'Wirrall Hill', the real name of the little rise, meaning only 'the hill of the bog-myrtle meadow'. The famous Glastonbury Thorn, botanists tell us, was simply a freakish form of common hawthorn; similar specimens have been known in other places, and the first clear allusion to it is on a fourteenth-century seal of the Abbey.

But here ends the havoc wrought on the legend by implacable historians. After all, Glastonbury needs no legend, however ethereal, however romantic, to enhance its venerable antiquity, for in essence, if not in detail, the story of the abbey as told by William of Malmesbury is true. That Glastonbury was the most venerated of all British shrines when the English invaders reached it, is beyond dispute, and the reason for this veneration was immense antiquity. We need not doubt that scores of Celtic saints came here to worship, and that many stayed. There is no inherent improbability in the visits of St. Patrick, St. Bridget, St. Gildas and St. David. Whether it was, or was not, St. Patrick who organised the Glastonbury hermits into the first monastery, the use of his name indicates at least, that the abbey was founded in the fifth century by Irish missionaries on a site already Christian, and this surprises no historian of the age. Perhaps the story of St. Philip's mission in the year 63 was invented by defiant Celtic clergy, struggling to assert their independence against the arrogant St. Augustine of Canterbury at the beginning of the seventh century, by claiming an origin independent of Rome and a founder co-equal with St. Peter. Although, like William of Malmesbury, we may withhold belief in so early an origin for Christian Glastonbury, the story has a core of probable truth. The later legend makes St. Joseph come to Glastonbury from the south-west. Take this in conjunction with St. Philip's fabled mission, and have we not here, despite all the forgotten detail, a half-conscious memory of a vitally important fact? To those familiar with the trend of recent research on early British Christianity, there will be no surprise in the suggestion conveyed by the Glastonbury legend, that Christianity, like so many prehistoric beliefs, came to Britain from the south-west—not by the short sea-route across the Dover Straits to London, but by the stormy western sea-ways between Brittany and Cornwall. Under Glastonbury Tor it may well have found its first resting-place and shelter in our land.

* * *

SUGGESTIONS FOR FURTHER READING

The best recent book on the subject of this essay is by the late Dean of Wells, Dr. Joseph Armitage Robinson: *Two Glastonbury Legends—King Arthur and Joseph of Arimathea* (Cambridge, 1926). There are shorter and more popular, but still scholarly and reliable accounts, by the late Dr. Montague R. James; *Abbeys* (London, G.W.R., 1925) and by E. Foord, *Wells, Glastonbury and Cleeve* (*Cathedrals, Abbeys and Famous Churches Series*, edit. Gordon Home, 1925). The passage from Gerald of Wales, describing the supposed discovery of the bodies of Arthur and Guinevere, has been translated by Professor H. E. Butler in *The Autobiography of Giraldus Cambrensis* (1937). I do not know of any translation of William of Malmesbury's *De antiquitate Glastoniensis ecclesiæ*, but the Latin text has been edited by Thomas Hearne in *Adam de Domerham Historia de rebus gestis Glastoniensibus*, vol. i, pp. 1–122 (Oxford, 1727) and in Migne's *Patrologia Latina*, vol. clxxix (Paris, 1855). The account, however, which he copied into his *De gestis regum Anglorum libri quinque*, is included in John Sharpe's translation of that work, *The History of the Kings of England and The Modern History of William of Malmesbury* (1815); in J. A. Giles' translation (based on Sharpe's), *William of Malmesbury's Chronicle of the Kings of England* (*Bohn's Antiquarian Library*, 1847); and also in Joseph Stevenson's translation in *The Church Historians of England*, vol. iii, pt. i (1854); it is therefore possible to read an English version of William's original account of the history of Glastonbury.

IV

The Flood

SIR LEONARD WOOLLEY

THERE can be few stories more familiar to us
than that of the Flood. The word 'antediluvian' has passed into common speech, and Noah's
Ark is still one of the favourite toys of the children's
nursery.

The Book of Genesis tells us how the wickedness of
man was such that God repented Him that He had
made man upon the earth, and decided to destroy all
flesh; but Noah, being the one righteous man, found
grace in the eyes of the Lord. So Noah was bidden by
God to build an ark, and in due time he and all his
family went in, with all the beasts and the fowls of the
air, going in two by two; and the doors of the ark were
shut and the rain was upon the earth for forty days and
forty nights, and the floods prevailed exceedingly and
the earth was covered, and all flesh that moved upon
the earth died, and Noah only remained alive and they
that were with him in the ark. And then the floods
abated. Noah sent out a raven and a dove, and at
last the dove brought him back an olive leaf, proof that
the dry land had appeared. And they all went forth
out of the ark, and Noah built an altar and offered
sacrifice, and the Lord smelt a sweet savour and
promised that never again would He smite everything

living, as He had done; and God set His bow in the
clouds as a token of the covenant that there should not
any more be a flood to destroy the earth.

For many centuries, indeed until only a few genera-
tions ago, the story of Noah was accepted as an historical
fact; it was part of the Bible, it was the inspired Word
of God, and therefore every word of it must be true.
To deny the story was to deny the Christian faith.

Then two things happened. On the one hand
scholars, examining the Hebrew text of Genesis, discovered that it was a composite narrative. There had
been two versions of the Flood story which differed in
certain small respects, and these two had been skilfully
combined into one by the Jewish scribes four or five
hundred years before the time of Christ, when they
edited the sacred books of their people and gave to them
the form which they have to-day. That discovery
shook the faith of many old-fashioned believers, or was
indignantly denied by them; they said that it was an
attack on the Divine Word. Really, of course, it was
nothing of the sort. Genesis is an historical book, and
the writer of history does not weave the matter out of
his imagination; he consults older authorities of every
sort and quotes them as freely and as often as may be.
The older the authorities are, and the more his account
embodies theirs, the more reason we have to trust what
he writes; if it be insisted that his writings are divinely
inspired, the answer is that 'inspiration' consists not in
dispensing with original sources but in making the right
use of them. The alarm felt by the orthodox when
confronted with the discoveries of scholarship was a
false alarm.

The second shock came when from the ruins of the
ancient cities of Mesopotamia archæologists unearthed

clay tablets on which was written another version of the Flood story—the Sumerian version. According to that, mankind had grown wicked and the gods in council decided to destroy the human race which they had made. But one of the gods happened to be a good friend of one mortal man, so he went down and warned him of what was to happen and counselled him to build an ark. And the man did so; and he took on board all his family, and his domestic animals, and shut the door, and the rain fell and the floods rose and covered all the earth. At last the storms abated and the ark ran aground, and the man sent out a dove and a swallow and a raven, and finally came forth from the ark and built an altar and did sacrifice, and the gods (who had had no food since the Flood started and were terribly hungry) 'came round the altar like flies', and the rainbow is set in the clouds as a warrant that never again will the gods destroy all men by water.

It is clear that this is the same story as we have in Genesis. But the Sumerian account was actually written before the time of Moses (whom some people had, without reason, thought to be the author of Genesis), and not only that, but before the time of Abraham. Therefore the Flood story was not by origin a Hebrew story at all but had been taken over by the Hebrews from the idolatrous folk of Babylonia; it was a pagan legend, so why should we for a moment suppose that it was true? All sorts of attempts were made to show that the Bible story was independent, or was the older of the two, but all the attempts were in vain, and to some it seemed as if the battle for the Old Testament had been lost.

Once more, it was a false alarm. Nobody had ever supposed that the Flood had affected only the Hebrew people; other people had suffered by it, and a disaster of such magnitude was bound to be remembered in their traditions; in so far as the Sumerian legend was closer in time to the event, it might be said to strengthen rather than to weaken the case for the Biblical version. But it could well be asked, 'Why should we believe a Sumerian legend which is, on the face of it, a fantastic piece of pagan mythology?' It is perfectly true that the Sumerian Flood story is a religious poem. It reflects the religious beliefs of a pagan people just as the biblical story reflects the religious beliefs of the Hebrews; and we cannot accept the Sumerian religion as true. Also, it is a poem, and everybody knows what poets are! Shakespeare certainly did:

> The poet's eye, in a fine frenzy rolling,
> Doth glance from heaven to earth, from earth to heaven,
> And, as imagination bodies forth
> The forms of things unknown, the poet's pen
> Turns them to shapes, and gives to airy nothing
> A local habitation and a name.

But the legend does not stand alone. Sober Sumerian historians wrote down a sort of skeleton of their country's history in the form of a list of its kings (like our 'William I, 1066', and all that); starting at the very beginning there is a series of perhaps fabulous rulers, and, they say, 'Then came the Flood. And after the Flood kingship again descended from heaven'; and they speak of a dynasty of kings who established themselves in the city of Kish, and next of a dynasty whose capital was Erech. Here, at least, we are upon historic ground, for archæological excavation in modern times has recovered the material civilisation of those ancient days when Erech was indeed the chief city of Mesopotamia. The old historians were sure that not long before these days the course of their country's history had been interrupted by a great flood. If they were right, it does not, of course, mean that the Flood legend is correct in all its details, but it does at least give it a basis of fact.

In the year 1929, when we had been digging at Ur the famous 'royal graves' with their extraordinary treasures, which can be dated to something like 2800 B.C., I determined to test still lower levels so as to get an idea of what might be found by digging yet deeper. We sank a small shaft below the stratum of soil in which the graves lay, and went down through the mixed rubbish that is characteristic of an old inhabited site—a mixture of decomposed mud-brick, ashes and broken pottery, very much like what we had been finding higher up. Then suddenly it all stopped: there were no more pot-sherds, no ashes, only clean, water-laid mud, and the workman in the shaft told me that he had reached virgin soil; there was nothing more to be found, and he had better go elsewhere.

I got down and looked at the evidence and agreed with him; but then I took my levels and found that 'virgin soil' was not nearly as deep down as I expected. That upset a favourite theory of mine, and I hate having my theories upset except on the very best of evidence, so I told him to get back and go on digging. Most unwillingly he did so, turning up nothing but clean soil that contained no sign of human activity; he worked down through eight feet of it and then, suddenly, flint implements appeared and sherds of painted pottery which, we were fairly sure, was the earliest pottery made in southern Mesopotamia (Plates 9 and 10). I was convinced of what it meant, but I wanted to see whether others would arrive at the same conclusion. I brought up two of my staff and, after pointing out the facts, asked for their conclusions. They did not know what to say. My wife came along and looked and was asked the same question, and she turned away, remarking quite casually, 'Well, of course, it's the Flood'.

So it was. But one could scarcely argue for the Deluge on the strength of a shaft a yard square; so the next season I marked out on the low ground where the graves had been a rectangle some seventy-five feet by sixty, and there dug a huge pit which went down, in the end, for sixty-four feet. The level at which we started had been the ground surface about 2600 B.C. Almost immediately we came on the ruins of houses slightly older than that; we cleared them away and found more houses below them. In the first twenty feet we dug through no fewer than eight sets of houses, each of which had been built over the ruins of the age before. Then the house ruins stopped and we were digging through a solid mass of potsherds wherein, at different levels, were the kilns in which the pots had been fired; the sherds represented those pots which went wrong in the firing and, having no commercial value, had been smashed by the potter and the bits left lying until they were so heaped up that the kilns were buried and new kilns had to be built. It was a vase factory which was running for so long a time that by the stratified sherds we could trace the course of history: near the bottom came the wares in use when Erech was the royal city, and at the very bottom was the painted ware of the land's earliest immigrants. And then came the clean, water-laid mud, eleven feet of it, mud which on analysis proved to be the silt brought down by the River Euphrates from its upper reaches hundreds of miles away; and under the silt, based on what really was

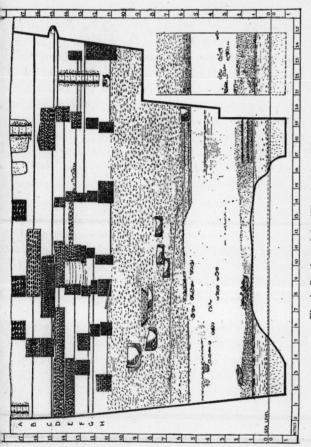

Fig. i. Section of the 'Flood-pit' at Ur.

The al 'Ubaid I house stratum begins at 1.00 m. above sea level. Between 1.50 m. and 5.50 m. is the Flood silt in which are graves of periods al 'Ubaid II and III. Between 5.50 m. and 11.00 m. is the stratum of kiln 'wasters', the pottery changing from al 'Ubaid II through Uruk to Jamdat Nasr. The date of stratum A is about 2600 B.C.

virgin soil, the ruins of the houses that had been over-whelmed by the flood and buried deep beneath the mud carried by its waters (Fig. i).

This was the evidence we needed; a flood of a magnitude unparalleled in any later phase of Meso-potamian history; and since, as the pottery proved, it had taken place some little while before the time of the Erech dynasty, this was the Flood of the Sumerian king-lists and that of the Sumerian legend and that of Genesis.

We have proved that the Flood really happened; but that does not mean that all the details of the Flood legend are true—we did not find Noah and we did not find his ark! But take a few details. The Sumerian version says (this is not mentioned in Genesis) that antediluvian man lived in huts made of reeds; under the Flood deposit we found the wreckage of reed huts. Noah built his ark of light wood and bitumen. Just on top of the Flood deposit we found a big lump of bitumen, bearing the imprint of the basket in which it had been carried, just as I have myself seen the crude bitumen from the pits of Hit on the middle Euphrates being put in baskets for export downstream. I reckoned that to throw up an eleven-foot pile of silt against the mound on which the primitive town of Ur stood the water would have to be at least twenty-five feet deep; the account in Genesis says that the depth of the flood water was fifteen cubits, which is roughly twenty-six feet. 'Twenty-six feet?' you may say; 'that's not much of a flood!' Lower Mesopotamia is so flat and low-lying that a flood having that depth at Ur would spread over an area 300 miles long and 100 miles wide.

Noah's Flood was not a universal deluge; it was a vast

flood in the valley of the Rivers Tigris and Euphrates. It drowned the whole of the habitable land between the eastern and the western deserts; for the people who lived there that was all the world. It wiped out the villages and exterminated their inhabitants, and although some of the towns set upon mounds survived, it was but a scanty and dispirited remnant of the nation that watched the waters recede at last. No wonder that they saw in this disaster the gods' punishment of a sinful generation and described it as such in a great religious poem; and if, as may well have been the case, one household managed to escape by boat from the drowned lowlands, the head of that house would naturally be made the hero of the saga.

SUGGESTIONS FOR FURTHER READING

The ancient cuneiform tablets giving the legend of the Flood were first translated by George Smith; his book, *The Chaldean Account of Genesis*, edited by A. H. Sayce in 1880, is probably the most easily accessible for most English readers and, old as it is, still serves its purpose very well. In comparing this with the Biblical account it has to be remembered that the latter combines two somewhat different versions, and the story becomes more intelligible if it be studied in the light of, for instance, S. R. Driver's *Introduction to the Literature of the Old Testament* (1898). The archæological evidence from Ur is given in full in the forthcoming Volume IV of *Ur Excavations*, 'The Early Periods'; a fairly detailed summary has appeared in the *Antiquaries Journal* for October 1930, Vol. X, No. 4, and my *Excavations at Ur* (Ernest Benn, 1954) tells the complete story. The 'king list' which I have cited is printed in a good many books, amongst them Leonard King's *History of Sumer and Akkad* (1914), but my quotation gives all that is relevant to the subject.

1. Stonehenge: surviving upright of main trilithon

9. Examples of al 'Ubaid I pottery from Ur, dating from before the Flood

10. Ur of the Chaldees

Terracotta Figurines of the al 'Ubaid period, representing goddesses
worshipped before the Flood

12. Coin of 5th century, showing the Minotaur and the Labyrinth

11. The Throne Room in the Palace at Knossos

13. A gold and ivory *Torera* from Knossos

V

Theseus
and the Minotaur

CHARLES SELTMAN

IN far-off days, when Athens was just one of several
towns in Attica and not yet the capital, a certain
king of Athens named Ægeus, travelling in the land of
Argos, was hospitably entertained at the township of
Troezen by its overlord. Ægeus fell in love with this
same overlord's charming daughter Aithra, and before
he left, he hid a pair of sandals and a sword under a
big slab of rock. He told Aithra that if their child
should be male, she was to wait until the boy was strong
enough to lift the rock, whereupon he could don the
sandals and bring the sword to Athens in order to be
recognised by his father. The boy, who early showed
beauty, intelligence and strength, was given the name
of Theseus. In due time he lifted the rock and set out
for Athens. Passing through the Bad Lands and over-
coming a variety of Bad Men, he won the reputation
of being a hero.

But when Theseus at last reached Athens, he found
the town in a state of deep gloom. For the third time
the people were expecting from Crete the collectors of
the living tribute of boys and girls for Minos. A few
years previously a son of Minos had—so Minos said—

been treacherously killed in Attica, and the king of Knossos harassed the land; the Athenians could obtain no peace until they agreed to this humiliating tribute. So once a year the collectors came and chose from among the Athenian people the seven most handsome youths and the seven most beautiful girls. These were carried off to Knossos, where Minos had built a great labyrinth, in the centre of which dwelt a monster of dire appearance, having the body of a powerful man and the head of a bull. He was called Minotauros, meaning 'bull of Minos', or as we say, Minotaur. The seven boys and seven girls were turned into the labyrinth where they wandered helplessly until one by one they chanced on the inner chamber, where they were devoured by the Minotaur.

When Theseus heard all this he placed himself among the eligible youths whom the collectors inspected. Naturally they first chose this young man who in stature, strength and appearance surpassed all his fellows. King Ægeus was much upset at the prospect of losing his newly-found son so quickly, but was encouraged by the assurance Theseus gave that he would kill the monster. Now the ship which carried the young victims to their doom sailed under a sheet of black canvas in mourning for the condemned. Ægeus persuaded his son to pack a white sail so that, if he were successful, the ship on its return might hoist the sail of happiness and good fortune.

Arrived at the great palace of Knossos, the company were well received by King Minos. And here we meet one of the first examples in history of romance, for King Minos' beautiful daughter, Ariadne, fell in love with Prince Theseus. Well aware of his peril, she met him at night by the entrance to the labyrinth, giving him a sword and, more important, a large ball of thread, one end of which she attached to a nail at the entrance. What use, she thought, to slay the Minotaur if her hero should never find his way out again? So Theseus unwound the thread, got to the centre of the great maze and, after a fearful fight, killed the monster. Then, following his clue by winding up the thread again, he regained the entrance and the arms of Ariadne.

At this point there are variations in the numerous different accounts of what happened. One of the better versions claims that after they had stove in the bottoms of King Minos' ships in the harbour of Knossos, Theseus, Ariadne, the seven youths and seven girls set sail due north and disembarked for the night on the island of Naxos. Now the idea of creating a splendid, romantic and faultless hero would have been repugnant to the Greeks, who were fully aware of the follies of mankind. They knew that every great man may be part hero and part cad and that even Theseus was as bad as the rest of them. Anyhow, having decided that he no longer needed her, this hero crept away from the sleeping Ariadne and set sail again with all his Athenian companions. Fortunately for the distracted girl the god Dionysos turned up next day all ready to console her, and she discovered that a god is a far better companion than any hero.

But in his haste to abandon the girl who had enabled him to kill the Minotaur, Theseus forgot his promise to his father Ægeus about hoisting the white sail. The old man, knowing the day when the ship should return, was perched high on a cliff where he could look south across the Cretan Sea, and presently he saw far off a ship with a black sail. Unable to bear this final grief, the old king cast himself down into the sea, which has ever since been called the Ægean Sea. The wicked sometimes flourish like the green bay-tree; and so indeed do the foolish and the careless, among whom Theseus must be classed. He was very upset at his father's death and provided all the funeral obsequies due to a dead king. But Theseus, slayer of the Minotaur, saviour of Athens, became its king; and it was he, so later writers said, who first united Attica into a single country, collecting most of the people into the one township of Athens, which thus became a city and the capital of the land of Attica.

Such is the general account of the conflict between Athens and Knossos—between Greece and Crete—which grew into one of the most charming romances ever told by men and women. But no Homer wove the tale of this war into a matchless epic, and the stories about it have come down to us in fragmentary allusions which have to be picked up and pieced together from a variety of references. And it would be wrong to leave out of account at least one other version according to which Theseus—far from sailing with the other youths and the girls as tribute—built a fleet secretly; some ships in a smugglers' harbour, and other ships away at Troezen, where he had been born. Sailing with these secret ships he surprised the Cretan fleet, destroyed it and captured Knossos.

Myth or Legend? What do the stories mean? Is there a background of historical fact behind them? In Chapter II Professor Page writes about Schliemann, whose belief in the reality of ancient Troy and single-minded devotion to the idea of finding the city of Priam, gave the world such great results. After his discovery of Troy, Schliemann once had the intention of digging at Knossos. With his extraordinary flair he identified the site, but political difficulties proved insuperable—the island of Crete was then in Turkish possession—and the actual discovery and the excavation of Knossos was carried out by another archæologist, Sir Arthur Evans. In the 1890's Evans spent some years travelling in Crete collecting evidence of prehistoric script which appeared on ancient sealstones. Then in 1894, by judicious purchase of fields and vineyards above the hidden ruins, he gained a foothold on the site. But politics still interfered until in 1897 patriotic Greek risings and Turkish severity resulted in action by the Protecting Powers, who made Crete into an independent state with Prince George of Greece as High Commissioner. Consequently, in 1900 Evans was able to begin the systematic excavation of the Palace of Minos at Knossos.

Knossos lies in the midst of a great seismic centre, and as far back as the evidence goes, one sees that earthquake after earthquake from 2000 to 1400 B.C. laid the buildings low. But they rose again from their ruins more splendid than before, until the final disaster from which there was no rebirth. At its greatest period the Palace rose many stories in height, and it soon became evident to Sir Arthur that these floors must, when possible, be preserved. Door-jambs, column-bases and floor-blocks, which had fallen into the rooms below, were raised to their proper levels, and concrete beams replaced the charred wooden originals which were discovered. Without restoration the Palace would have been a meaningless heap melting away under the sun and the rains of Crete. As it now stands, its magnitude and grandeur, the elegance of its staircases, corridors and bathrooms, can only astonish.

The visitor soon observes in a variety of places the
sign of the Double-axe, a weapon known as the *labrys*
in ancient times. This sign resembles two equal
isosceles triangles having a common apex through
which runs a line representing the haft of the weapon.
Greeks of the classical age, who could still see the
remains of the ruined Palace, could also observe the
labrys symbol, so they called the place the 'labyrinth',
or the *House of the Labrys*. Anyone who has looked
down from the top of a bus upon a heavily blitzed area
has realised how very like a maze foundation walls may
be. The Palace of Minos looked like that, and the
word 'labyrinth' came to mean the maze.

Forty years after he began to dig, Sir Arthur Evans
reported: 'The work of the spade has now brought out
the essential underlying truth of the old traditions that
made Knossos the most ancient centre of civilised life
in Greece and with it, of our whole Continent. No
equal plot of Earth's surface has been productive in
such various directions of so many unique records
bearing on our earliest culture'. What else, one may
ask, has been discovered, besides the labyrinth, to link
up with the Athenian story of Theseus? How much
of that fable is founded in history?

There are three further discoveries which deserve
our attention. Firstly, there is a number of ancient
Cretan sealstones, having an engraved picture of a man
with a bull-mask covering his face and head; a man
who may be enacting a religious dance or ceremony.
It is certain that classical Greeks knew of similar seals
since they actually copied them for coins in the fifth
century B.C. (Plate 11). Those seals are quite enough
to explain the invention of the Minotaur.

Secondly, the ancient inhabitants of Knossos before

Fig. ii. Fresco found at Knossos depicting a bull and young athletes.

1400 B.C. had a passion for the bull-ring, and the excavations have produced pictures and statuettes that provide complete information about the sport. Athletic youths and girls acted as Toreros and Toreras. When the bull charged, the young athlete grabbed its horns and was tossed so as to make a back-somersault over the bull's spine. Here is surely the explanation of the strange fable about the annual tribute exacted from Athens of seven youths and seven girls destined for the 'bull of Minos'. They were not given as fodder to a monster, but trained to desport themselves in the bull-ring at Knossos to make a Cretan holiday (Fig. ii and Plate 12, facing p. 49).

Thirdly, the rich, spacious Palace and the large city of Knossos itself were unwalled. At a time when residences and townships in every other Mediterranean land or island were heavily fortified, those of Crete alone remained open and undefended. Only one thing could make this possible—an unconquered fleet in total control of the seas. Archæological discovery has given proof of something like a far-flung Minoan naval empire, the influence of which extended from Sicily to all Southern Greece, to all the islands of the Ægean Sea, to the coastal lands of Asia Minor and to Cyprus. The folk of Knossos could sleep peacefully in their beds because Minos ruled the waves. But suppose that a large part of the fleet were absent, and that a clever subject king of Minos with a small secret fleet could surprise the remaining Minoan ships in port, destroy them, land and sack the Palace. Suppose Pearl Harbour had been the harbour of New York—what then? It is here that we begin to perceive that the fables about Theseus may be founded on the actualities of history. Was it the Athenian Theseus who put an end to the Minoan civilisation? The various tales about him point to his control of all the coasts near Athens. Perhaps he began to realise that his new kingdom was powerful, that he had dependable allies, and that, with their help, Cretan power could be destroyed. Economically the Greeks might benefit from such an event, and there was justification for attack because the annual tribute of boys and girls sent to Knossos was both exasperating and humiliating.

In Athens centuries later a yearly ceremony took place which was linked up with the Theseus legend, and it was assumed that Theseus sailed for Crete late in April or early in May. Now, it has been remarked that there are marks of fire on the western front of the Palace at Knossos, where blazing beams of wood collapsed during the sack of the great building. A violent south wind carried the smoke from this fire northward; and even to-day it is only late in April or early in May that so strong a south wind blows in Crete. When these two facts are put together it seems as though we know the time of year when Knossos was destroyed,

but of course not the actual date. As witness for the
suddenness of the destruction, we have only to observe
what has been called the most dramatic room on any
ancient site—the Throne Room—where, between
painted griffins on the wall, the Throne of Minos still
stands (Plate 13 pp. 48–9).

When this room was first revealed by the spades
of the excavators, overturned jars and ritual vessels
testified to confusion and panic, as if the King
himself had felt obliged to perform or to suffer some
final secret rite for the salvation of his people. Those
ancient sealstones suggest that at times a man might
have a ritual bull-mask over his face and head. Did
the King, in these final moments, wear such a mask?
Was it a king disguised as a Minotaur whom Theseus
slew?

SUGGESTIONS FOR FURTHER READING

The great work on this subject is by Sir Arthur Evans,
The Palace of Minos, Vols. I–IV, and Index (1922–37).
Much information can also be obtained from the two
following books by J. D. S. Pendlebury: *The Archæology of
Crete* (1939), and *A Handbook to the Palace of Minos at
Knossos* (1933); and there is an excellent collection of
pictures in H. T. Bossert's *The Art of Ancient Crete* (1937).
In *History Today*, Volume II, Numbers 4 and 5 (April and
May, 1952) there are articles by Charles Seltman on Life
in Ancient Crete, the second of which is concerned with
the connexion between Crete and Atlantis. The most
recent account, for the general reader, of the discoveries
of Schliemann and Evans is L. Cottrell, *The Bull of Minos*,
with an Introduction by Professor Wace (1953).

VI

Tara

SEÁN P. Ó RÍORDÁIN

IN the nineteenth century the poet Moore wrote:

> The harp that once through Tara's halls
> The soul of music shed
> Now hangs as mute on Tara's walls
> As if that soul were fled.

His theme was lament for departed glory. So in the eighteenth century an unknown poet writing in Irish, notes how time has defeated Alexander and Cæsar and the city of Troy, and couples with them deserted Tara. 'Grass grows on Tara, Troy is overthrown,' he writes. Troy and Tara, Cæsar and Alexander, are for him figures of greatness departed.

Past glory, past greatness are symbolised by Tara. It is also a site which awakens the affection of the Irish people. Scarcely a day passes but Tara has its visitors. On the Sunday before St. Patrick's Day, numbers of people will come, as I saw them do twelve months ago, to pick shamrock on the Hill of Tara—for clearly Tara's shamrock is hallowed by the soil from which it grew.

For those who know something of archæology the monuments on the Hill of Tara are of interest; for those who have no such background knowledge the site may be, quite frankly, a disappointment. In the absence of great buildings or impressive ruins, the hill itself, magnificent though the prospect is, of the richest lands of the central plain of Ireland, cannot account for the attraction of the site, and certainly not for the awe and reverence among people throughout Ireland and among exiles, many of whom have never seen and never hope to see the Hill of Tara (Plate 14 facing p. 64).

Let us look to the reason.   Ireland is rich in sites of which there are accounts in the early history as recorded in ancient manuscripts.   Let us take it for the moment that many of these accounts must be thought of as 'history' in inverted commas.   The amount of such material varies considerably as between one site and another.   But Tara surpasses them all in the multiplicity of references to it and in the importance of its rôle in the early history of the country.   Further, while many of the places mentioned in early history or ancient tales are difficult to identify, or can only be identified provisionally, no one doubts that the Hill of Tara in County Meath is in fact identical with the ancient *Teamhair—Teamhair na Riogh*, Tara of the Kings, Royal Tara.

And there is the kernel of the whole story.   At Tara lived kings, and these were no provincial kings but were kings of Ireland: so their glory is the glory of early Ireland and their rule meant the unity of Ireland, and their seat at Tara symbolised that glory and that unity.

It would be quite impossible to present even in summary all the material related to Tara which the scribes have left us, but let us glance at some of it.   We are told that Tara was the chief residence of the Irish kings from the time of Sláinge, who reigned in the twentieth century B.C., and continued to be occupied until the reign of Diarmuid in the sixth century A.D., when the site was cursed by St. Ruadhán because of a quarrel between the king and the saint, and was deserted as a result. Sláinge would not be accepted by any present-day historian, nor would the story of King Diarmuid and St. Ruadhán be regarded as more than a fanciful way of recounting a clash between Church and State. But let us not be critical for the present, and let us see with what the scribes filled in the long period between the foundation of Tara and its desertion.

From its foundation until its abandonment in the sixth century there reigned at Tara, we are told, one hundred and forty-two monarchs, of whom one hundred and thirty-six were pagan and six were Christian. Certain of these monarchs are remarkable for their contributions to the development of Tara. The fortieth in the succession (in the thirteenth century B.C.) was Ollamh Fodhla, so named because of his wisdom; for *Ollamh* means a learned one, and he established the assembly known as the Feis of Tara, held every third year, at the feast of *Samhain*, corresponding to our Hallowe'en. The foundation of this great assembly was a notable achievement; for this Feis continues to be spoken of as a national function throughout the history of Tara and it is described by early and later writers. Thus the seventeenth-century historian Keating writes:

'Now the Feis of Tara was a great general assembly like a parliament in which the nobles and scholars of Ireland . . . were wont to lay down and to renew rules and laws and to approve the annals and records of Ireland. There, too, it was arranged that each of the nobles of Ireland should have a

seat according to his rank and title.' And he goes
on to say ' . . . it was also their custom to pass six
days in feasting together . . . making peace and
entering into friendly alliances.'

Many of the kings in the regnal lists are mere names
and little or nothing is recounted of them. But Tuathal
in the second century A.D. is the central figure of several
tales intimately connected with the story of Tara.
Tuathal, son of a king of Tara, was born in Britain,
where his mother had taken refuge after his father had
been slain by the rebellious vassal tribes. At the age of
twenty-five Tuathal returned with a great host, rallied
his supporters in Ireland and established himself at
Tara. To him is ascribed the foundation of the
kingdom of Meath and the building in it of four
palaces—one of which was at Tara.

In the third century A.D. we meet with the most
notable of the names of the kings of Tara—Cormac mac
Airt. A wise judgment which he gave brought him to
the throne, and his reign is regarded as a golden age
during which Tara reached the summit of its glory,
and the ancient writers compare him with Solomon.

In Cormac's time many of the buildings of Tara
were erected, including the most magnificent of all
—the great Banqueting Hall. Bringing artificers from
across the sea, he built at Tara the first water-mill
known in Ireland. In his time there flourished Finn
mac Cumhaill and his warriors, and connected with
Cormac and Finn is the great Irish love-tale concerning
Gráinne, daughter of Cormac, who was promised to
Finn but who eloped with his lieutenant Diarmuid. To
Tara came Finn and his warriors to ask for Gráinne as
Finn's wife, and from Tara Gráinne and Diarmuid
eloped to begin their epic wanderings which end in

Diarmuid's death. At Tara is a site named from Gráinne, and the joint names of Diarmuid and Gráinne attached to megalithic tombs throughout Ireland bear witness to their flight.

In the fourth century the kings of Tara frequently raided Roman Britain, and one of them, Eochu, brought back from there the woman who was to become his wife. Their son, Niall of the Nine Hostages, continued the raiding with vigour, and it was he who brought back among his captives the boy who was to be St. Patrick, the Apostle of Ireland. From Niall are descended the Uí Néill, a family who provided all except two of the kings of Ireland down to the early eleventh century.

Niall died on one of his raids about A.D. 427, and was succeeded by his son Laoghaire, in whose reign occurred one of the most momentous happenings in the history of Tara—the coming of St. Patrick as a missionary. Laoghaire refused to be converted and, when he died fighting the Leinstermen, he was buried in pagan fashion in his fort at Tara, standing upright with his weapons facing his Leinster enemies.

Patrick's coming to Tara was the beginning of the end. We have heard of the cursing of Tara in the sixth century. After that there were still kings of Tara, but there is no certainty that they lived at the site from which they took their title.

Such in brief is the story. Before we try to evaluate it, let us look at the site itself. The Hill of Tara, about twenty miles to the north of Dublin, is not a great eminence. It is a north-south ridge rising to about 500 feet above sea-level, but remarkable for the prospect it commands over the plain on which it is set. On the hill we find a series of earthworks of various types—

burial mounds, circular enclosures and, at the north, two great parallel banks. Most of the individual sites are now marked with plaques which give the names by which they have been identified—the Fort of the Kings, Cormac's House, The Royal Seat, the Fort of the Synods and so on. The identifications are based on a medieval tract known as the *Dinnshenchas*, in which the notable places in early Ireland are described and in which Tara is given pride of place. Not only are the Tara sites named in the tract, but their position is given in relation to each other.

So we find the burial mound known as the Mound of the Hostages, the small ring-forts known as Cormac's House, the Royal Seat and Gráinne's Rath, the larger fort named from King Laoghaire, the great enclosure named the Fort of the Kings, and a site with concentric banks which is the Fort of the Synods. Most remarkable of all are the two parallel banks, over seven hundred feet long, labelled the *Teach Miodhchuarta* or Banquet Hall. For information on this hall we have as authority not only the *Dinnshenchas*, but also the plans of it which are given in two manuscripts—the twelfth-century *Book of Leinster* and the early fifteenth-century *Yellow Book of Lecan*. The plans show a rectangular building, divided into five long aisles, in which compartments are marked to show the various professions and grades of society appropriate to each. Beside the name of the occupants of each cubicle is given the joint of meat allotted to them at the banquet (Fig. iii and Plate 15).

Of the long story told of Tara, of the detailed ancient description of its monuments, how much may be accepted as reliable? How much is real history, how much myth, how much legend? The history of Tara

14. Tara: aerial view of the Fort of Kings, showing the Royal Seat and Cormac's House

15. Tara: the Banquet Hall from the south

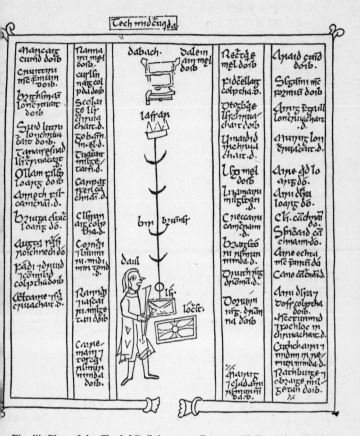

Fig. iii. Plan of the *Teach Miodhchuarta*, or Banquet Hall, as given in the twelfth century *Book of Leinster*. *After Royal Irish Academy reproduction (published 1880).*

The figure is a table attendant

is in essence the history of early Ireland, but much of the ancient story with its long regnal lists is not accepted by modern scholars. These lengthy royal pedigrees are neither myth nor legend, they are pseudo-history, fictitious pedigrees compiled by the ancient historians to give common royal ancestry to peoples of varying origin who came to Ireland at different times.

Scholars are not in agreement as to how much they would accept, but even one of our most critical authorities regards Tuathal as an historical personage. Instead of the tale of his Irish origin, Tuathal is argued to be leader of invaders who came to Ireland in the first century B.C. But it is held that Tuathal, when he established himself at Tara, found it to be already a royal seat.

At what date kings began to reside there history may not decide, but, even by these most critical standards, it has a respectable antiquity. Cormac mac Airt and his contemporary Finn have been declared to be fictions, and much of the magnificence of the description of Cormac's Banqueting Hall is thought to be copied from Biblical accounts of Solomon's temple. From the late fourth century, however, the names of the kings are accepted.

Archæologists have suggested a remote antiquity for the origin of Tara—based in part on the discovery there of Bronze Age finds, including the two great gold torques now in the National Museum of Ireland. But the objects were found by chance, not in the course of any formal excavation, and they are not associated with any structure on the hill. As yet not much excavation has been done at Tara. Over fifty years ago the site known as the Rath of the Synods was dug by British-Israelite seekers for the Ark of the Covenant—though how they reasoned that it had been buried there is hard to imagine. They left no record of their diggings. Last summer systematic excavation on the same site showed that it was a complicated structure which had four building phases, and that its purpose was in part ritual. Central buildings were of wood, and wood was freely used to build the elaborate palisades which surrounded them. Roman type pottery and other Roman objects found were due in the main to contacts with Roman Britain, but in part also with Roman Gaul.

The ritual function mentioned in connexion with this site emphasises the religious character of Tara. St. Patrick's coming to Tara is described by his biographer as a visit to 'the chief seat of idolatry and druidism of Erin'. On the archæological indications, ritual, burial and habitation are represented by the earthworks on the hill. These are the material evidences of the history of Tara—evidence of rulers and of pagan priests. The stone known as the Lia Fail, we are picturesquely told, uttered a cry beneath the feet of the king. The old *Dinnshenchas* account would indicate that many other monuments formerly existed and, if in the abundance of sites named we are sometimes doubtful of the identification of those that remain, we still find sufficient to substantiate the importance of Tara.

Even if the scribes stole from Solomon's temple to embellish Tara's Hall, the great banks are there to mark the site. If excavations reveal that this is indeed the hall, it should prove it to be one of the greatest prehistoric buildings in western Europe.

On the material side it will be possible to give a more complete answer to the question 'myth or legend' when, for several more seasons, excavation has gone on in the slow, patient way of present-day archæology.

Already on one site we have evidence of the wooden buildings that stood there. If in imagination we visualise many buildings also of wood, which stood on other earthworks, the hill becomes alive, and we see it a fitting centre for royal court and religious ritual.

A further season's excavation (Summer 1953) on the Rath of the Synods has confirmed the findings of 1952. Additional Roman material was found, and a date is indicated for the site extending from the first to the late third century A.D. Evidence was obtained for ordinary domestic and industrial activity as well as for a ritual use.

SUGGESTIONS FOR FURTHER READING

George Petrie: 'On the History and Antiquities of Tara Hill', *Transactions of the Royal Irish Academy*, Vol. XVIII, pp. 25–232, and published as book (Dublin, 1839).

Edward Gwynn: 'The metrical Dindsenchas', Part 1, *Royal Irish Academy Todd Lecture Series*, Vol. VIII (1903), pp. 2–45, 57–79.

R. A. S. Macalister: 'Teamhair Breg: A study of the Remains and Traditions of Tara', *Proceedings of the Royal Irish Academy*, Vol. XXXIV (1919), 231–399.

R. A. S. Macalister: *Tara: A Pagan Sanctuary of Ancient Ireland*, (London, 1931).

Two short guides to the Hill of Tara are: R. A. S. Macalister: *Tara*. No date. (Price 3d.) S. P. Ó Ríordáin: *Tara: The Monuments on the Hill*. Dundalk, 1954 (Price 2/6). (The illustrations here represented on Plate 14 and page 65 are from this booklet by courtesy of Dundalgan Press (W. Tempest) Ltd.)

VII

Tristan and Isolt

JON MANCHIP WHITE

'TO tell the joys that were betwixt la Beale Isoud
and Sir Tristram, there is no tongue can tell it,
nor heart think it, nor pen write it.'

So wrote Sir Thomas Malory. In the face of such
a comment, he is a bold man who attempts to relate
the story—'no tongue can tell it, nor pen write it'.
But it is probably true that, except for Romeo and
Juliet, Tristan and Isolt are the most famous pair of
lovers in literature. Their story is most familiar to us
to-day in the pages of Malory himself and the music
of Richard Wagner, but there are scores of other
modern and medieval versions of the classic legend.

First, I propose to tell the tale in the form in which it
comes down to us from the hands of early French and
German authors.

Tristan is the nephew of King Mark of Cornwall,
and his uncle's special favourite. At the time of the
story, Cornwall is tributary to the Kingdom of Ireland,
and every three years King Mark is compelled to send
to Ireland a melancholy cargo of thirty youths and
thirty maidens.

Like Theseus of old, the chivalrous young hero
decides to put an end to this monstrous impost. When
the mountainous brother of the Queen of Ireland comes
to demand the tribute, Tristan challenges him to single

combat and kills him; but during the course of the fight Tristan himself is wounded—by a poisoned sword. The Queen is the only person who can cure the festering wound, so Tristan travels to Ireland in the guise of a wandering minstrel, hiding his identity under the name of Tantris. The device of travelling incognito by simply reversing the syllables of one's name may seem rather naïve, but in the sixth century it obviously served its turn. At any event, the Queen fails to recognise the personable young troubadour as the slayer of her brother, and with the help of her daughter Isolt she nurses him back to health.

On his return to the court of Cornwall, he must have gossiped about the beauty of the Queen's daughter, for in a short while his uncle sends him back to Ireland to bring her to Britain as his bride and queen. Tristan dutifully claims her hand from the King of Ireland on behalf of his uncle, and the pair take ship for Cornwall. Probably they were already in love, or half in love; but their fate is sealed when they drink a love-potion which, by accident or design, has been left lying about by the princess's lady-in-waiting.

Opera-goers will recall how, as Wagner's passionate music ebbs and surges, the knight and the lady stand gazing with rapture at each other as the ship sweeps into harbour. And in the background can be heard the harsh and menacing shouts of the sailors: 'Hail to King Mark! Hail to King Mark!'

Isolt becomes Queen of Cornwall; and right from the beginning she deceives her elderly, doting husband with the young man whom he delights to honour. They meet secretly, many times. But at last the King receives unmistakable proof of their adultery, and condemns them to be burned alive.

When Tristan is being taken by his guards to the place of execution, he spies a chapel on the edge of a towering cliff, and begs the men-at-arms to allow him to enter and make a final prayer. Once inside he whips the bolt across the door, and hurls himself from the chapel window on to the soft sand of the beach below—a leap as tremendous, says the old French poet, as the distance from 'Costantin to Rome'.

Safe himself, Tristan rescues Isolt, and takes her to the forest of Morrois, where they lead a wild and idyllic existence, rather like Deirdre and Naoise after their flight from King Conchubar.

But at last the old and grieving King Mark persuades his young wife to return to him. He even persuades her to swear on holy relics that she has been faithful to him all along. His retinue sets out across the White Land to the place where the relics are housed, and at a ford which afterwards became known as *Le Mal Pas*— The False Step—a leper beggar suddenly appears, seizes the Queen and attempts to carry her across the water, only to trip and stumble with her half-way over. The leper beggar is Tristan in disguise, and although he is forced to take to his heels and leave his lover behind, the incident enables her to swear, with perfect truth, that the King and the beggar are the only two men who have ever embraced her.

Tristan now takes service abroad in what might literally be called a 'free-lance' capacity. At length he is badly wounded in battle in Brittany, and sends an urgent message for Isolt to come to him. He tells his messenger that if she is in the ship as it nears the coast of Brittany, he is to hoist a white sail; if she is not in the ship, he is to hoist a black one. The messenger duly hoists the white sail, but the mistress with whom

Tristan has been amusing himself in France is so jealous that she tells him, as he lies on his death-bed, that the sail she can see from the castle window is a black sail, and he dies of grief.

Isolt too, when she lands, dies of grief, and King Mark gives instructions that the bodies of the ill-starred lovers are to be brought back to Britain and buried in his own chapel. From the tomb of Tristan there springs a beautiful briar-rose, which droops over the tomb of Isolt and takes root there. And however often men cut it down, it always grows again and bends towards her tomb.

How much of this powerful, primitive story is, in origin true—a legend? Or is the whole of the enduring tale a fiction—a myth? No doubt most of the super-structure is the product of the story-teller's art, but we may be able to establish that its essential foundation is rooted in history, and that these roots may still be discerned.

First of all, is there any indication that the kingdoms of Cornwall and Ireland were linked in the manner described in the story? Yes, we know the Cornish and Irish peoples were closely associated with one another for well over a thousand years before King Mark and his nephew were born. It was Irish pioneers who first worked the tin lodes of Cornwall, at the very beginning of the Bronze Age. They sailed across the Irish Sea in frail boats and put ashore on the north coast of the peninsula. We can take it for granted that they avoided Land's End, with its snatching winds and snarling currents, like the plague. The voyage between southern Ireland and northern Cornwall was not only safer, but it was much shorter as well, and it is somewhere along that northern coast that we must look for the place of entry of the enchanted lovers.

The likeliest spot, in my opinion, is the port of Hale, which possesses a fine wide estuary. This was the natural port of entry for Irish visitors or invaders. And it was the terminal point of the old Bronze Age track-way that led south across the moors to Bodmin and Fowey. It was at Hale that Fingar landed with 'seven hundred and seventy bishops', after large-scale Irish incursions began in the fifth century. The incursions are attested in Cornwall by the presence of stones inscribed with the runic alphabet known as Ogham, found chiefly in Southern Ireland. The alphabet was introduced into Britain at the same period as the drama of Tristan and Isolt was being played out, proof positive that the two countries were in contact in the fashion indicated in the story.

From Hale the lovers would set out down the Bronze Age trackway, in a direction we can trace even to-day by means of the string of shattered stone pillars and crosses spaced out along its entire length.

It is beside one of these broken grey pillars, as we near the southern end of the trackway, that we must pause. The pillar stands at a cross-roads a mile and a half north of Fowey. It is over seven feet high and roughly square in section. And on one of its faces is an inscription in two vertical lines. Except for the first letter the script is Roman. The inscription reads: HIC IACIT DRUSTANS CUNOMORI FILIUS, 'Here lies Drustans, son of Cunomorus'. It is a strange sensation to put one's hand on the pitted surface of the ruined column and to know, beyond reasonable doubt, that one is laying one's hand on the tombstone of Tristan, Count of Lyonesse (Plate 16, facing p. 80).

Why should this stone be a monument to Tristan? The reading of the name *Drustans* has been disputed.

Langdon, chronicler of the Cornish crosses, read it as
Circusius. But most modern scholars would accept the
reading *Drustans*, which is identical philologically with
the name of *Tristan*.

But what about *Cunomorus*? Who was *he*? We know
from a biography of St. Paul Aurelian, written by a
Cornish monk, that this somewhat peppery saint had a
quarrel with a king of Cornwall called *Quonomorius*.
We also know that St. Paul sailed from Brittany to
Cornwall in the sixth century, the century in which
our tale occurred. Surely, then, *Cunomorus* is *Quonomorius*? Reading on, we find that the monk not only
wrote *Quonomorius* in his manuscript, but *Marcus dictus
Quonomorius*: 'Mark called Cunomorus.'

Why is Tristan called the *son* of Mark, when in the
story he is called the *nephew*? We can only guess that
the medieval story-teller hesitated, out of moral nicety,
from making a hero out of a man who seduced his
father's future bride. So close a relationship, allied to
so base a treachery, would lose the vital sympathy of
the audience. Tristan, called nephew, was Mark's son.

Now let us walk along the road from the Tristan
memorial for another mile and a half. We climb a
hill. The upland winds begin to sing in the telegraph
wires. As we climb, we leave behind us the leafy
tunnel of the cross-roads and move into bleaker terrain.
Away to our right stretches a magnificent view over
the estuary, dotted with the sails of the small craft
riding at anchor.

At last we halt beside the gate of a large cornfield,
sweeping majestically away downhill. At the top end
of the open field is a sombre and mysterious feature:
an isolated island of closely-set trees and bristling scrub,
four hundred feet long.

This dark rampart of trees and scrub is called Castle Dôr (Plate 17, facing p. 81).

Let us go through the five-barred gate into the corn-field and examine this curious castle more closely. But we must be careful how we advance through the outer defences of bramble and bracken, otherwise we shall find ourselves tumbling into an immense ditch, the bottom of which is strewn with boulders. We must inch our way cautiously to the edge of the crumbling fosse, where we can gaze across the broad chasm at the steep earthen rampart beyond.

Castle Dôr is a large circular earthwork. It was excavated by Mr. Ralegh Radford in 1936 and 1937. Earthworks of this class usually belong to the Early Iron Age, but they were often re-used by later builders. Ten miles away from Castle Dôr, at St. Denis, there is a charming little church inside another Iron Age fort.

Mr. Radford found that the earliest occupation of the fortress extended from the second century B.C. to the first century A.D. But a more spectacular discovery awaited him. He found the remains of a *second* occupation, dating from a period five or six centuries later. The second occupation took the form of a number of large buildings, whose design and dimensions exactly resembled the accounts given by early Irish and Welsh authors of the *dûn* or *llys* of a Celtic chieftain. He had found Lancien, the palace of Mark called Cunomorus, which medieval poets described as 'the strong and high city approached by an ancient road'.

We know from a medieval French writer that the name of the palace was *Lancien*, a word which we find written as *Lantien* in Domesday Book. Believe it or not, this word is still used to-day in the neighbourhood of Castle Dôr. Two miles away from the castle is a farm called *Lantine*. In his excavation report, Mr. Radford remarked that the farm is 'the humble successor of one of the great paramount manors of the Middle Ages'.

Linguistic parallels of this sort between early versions of the story and its Cornish background were made half a century ago by Loth, the French Celticist. The forest *Morrois*—may it not be the countryside in the neighbourhood of the modern manor of *Moresk*? *Le Mal Pas*—may it not be the modern ford at *Malpas*? The White Land—may it not be the manor of *Chirgwin*, Cornish for White Land? The downs at Chirgwin are strewn with white quartz, and Loth says that 'a great part of the manor is literally a White Plain'.

And what about the staggering leap from the chapel on the cliff, the leap from 'Costantin to Rome'? This is puzzling, perhaps, but quite straightforward: 'Constantin to Rome'—Constantinople to Rome. But *is* it? Could not the poet be corrupting the name of the village of *Constantine*, with its lovely church? Could not his *Rome* be a clerkish error for *Rame*? 'From Constantine to Rame Head'—the whole length of the southernmost stretch of the coast of Cornwall. Surely this homely simile sounds more accurate?

I hope I have said enough to convince you of the authentic Cornish setting of the famous tale. I hope, too, that I have not appeared to diminish the lovers by revealing them as they must have been—a pair of semi-barbarians—and by reducing turreted Lancien to the dimensions of a Kaffir kraal. The kindly king grieved just as sorely for Tristan because Lancien was a smaller palace than, say, Versailles. Isolt wept just as bitterly for him because he was laid to rest beneath a rough pillar, and not in a splendid tomb. It still gives one a strange feeling to look at the stone column and see the primitive inscription, with the provincial *iacit* instead of *iacet*, written in the old dead Roman tongue: DRUSTANS HIC IACIT CUNOMORI FILIUS.

Let us, as seems fitting, give the last word to an Irishman, William Butler Yeats; for the Butlers may well have some of the blood of the lovers in their veins, though all poets surely have a little:

> Sleep, beloved, such a sleep
> As did that wild Tristram know
> When, the potion's work being done,
> Roe could run or doe could leap
> Under oak and beechen bough
> Roe could leap or doe could run . . .

SUGGESTIONS FOR FURTHER READING

An expanded version of the present article was published in Volume III, Number 4 of *History Today* (April, 1953). The two papers which provided its essential basis were printed in the *Journal of the Royal Institution of Cornwall*, Volume XIX, Part 3 (1914), and Volume I of the New Series (Appendix 1951). The papers are by Henry Jenner and C. A. Ralegh Radford respectively. For the archæology of the period, the reader should consult H. O'Neill Hencken's volume on *Cornwall* in the Victoria County History library, one of the best contributions to this well-known series. For those who cannot obtain Sommer's edition or the great Oxford University Press edition of E. Vinaver, the most easily accessible edition of the *Morte d'Arthur* is that of Rhys in the Everyman Library. E. K. Chambers' *Arthur of Britain* (1927) offers a classic account of early British literature, including the Tristan literature, together with an invaluable bibliography.

VIII

St. George and the Dragon

E. R. LEACH

D RAGONS are not only large animals, they are
also a large subject. A learned German has
recorded over a thousand different versions of just one
dragon story, so you must not expect me to deal
comprehensively with the matter in just a few pages.

Of course everyone knows what dragons look like.
To quote expert authority: 'A dragon is a kind of
crocodile with something of the shape of a scorpion,
or perhaps of a lizard . . . he is generally a fire-
breather, and though sometimes he has only one head,
he more usually has either three, seven or nine. The
heads have the power of growing back again unless
they are all cut off at once.' To that I would merely
add that dragons are undoubtedly rather closely related
to snakes and pythons.

As with more normal zoological species, the behaviour of dragons is stereotyped and predictable, but
it is considerably affected by environment. Consequently, it has come to be supposed—mistakenly—
that there are several distinct species of dragon, such
as maiden-eating dragons, treasure-guarding dragons,
and royal ancestor dragons. Actually these three
behaviour patterns can all be found in one and the
same beast. There was a distinguished dragon called

Erichthonios, who lived on the Acropolis at Athens, and guarded the treasure-house of Athena. He was also noted for having attacked his virgin attendants and driven them mad, and for being the grandfather of one of the first kings of Athens.

St. George's dragon was a typical specimen of the maiden-eating variety. Here briefly is the story.

'Near the town of Silena in Lybia there was a pond infested by a dragon which sometimes approached the walls of the town and poisoned with his breath all who dwelt near. The citizens paid tribute to the monster. Each day a man or beast had to be offered, so that at last they gave up their children, sons and daughters, and none were spared. Finally, the lot fell on the King's daughter. The monarch, horror-struck, offered in exchange for her his gold, his silver, and half his realm, but to no avail. Just then St. George, who was a military tribune in the army of the Roman Emperor Diocletian, was passing through Silena and learned of the impending tragedy. He immediately mounted his horse and, armed with his lance, rushed to encounter the dragon, whom he reached just as the monster was about to devour the royal virgin. When St. George had overthrown the dragon, the princess fastened her girdle round the beast's neck and he followed her like a dog led on a leash. The inhabitants of Silena were so impressed by this remarkable sight that 20,000 of them were immediately baptized Christians, whereupon St. George struck off the head of the monster.'

But who was St. George? I regret to say that he appears to be almost as mythical as the monster he disposed of. The story goes that when martyred by Diocletian for refusing to abjure the Christian faith, he was put to death seven times in succession—by

Photo W. F. Ellis, Ltd

16. Tristan's Monument near Fowey

17. Aerial view of Castle Dôr

diverse ghastly means—but on each occasion, except the last, he was miraculously restored to health. It seems very doubtful whether there ever was an historical St. George. Some have tried to identify him with a certain Aryan Bishop of Alexandria who died in A.D. 362, but there exists in a church in Syria an inscription dated A.D. 346 in which St. George is already referred to as holy martyr. More frequently St. George has been identified as the nameless hero who, when the Emperor Diocletian issued his edicts against the Christians, rashly went round the city tearing down the notices. Naturally he was executed. Historical or not, St. George, as a saint, was very widely worshipped throughout the Near East from the third century onwards. His adoption as patron saint of England dates from the time of the Crusades.

The puzzle of course is this. How should an entirely fabulous saint manage to surround himself with such an extensive cult? The most likely answer is that the cult is earlier than St. George. There is very satisfactory evidence that around the tenth century A.D. the stories told about St. George's martyrdom were almost identical to those told about the death of Adonis, a god belonging to an earlier era altogether. Those of you who have read Sir James Frazer's *Golden Bough* will know that the story of the death and resurrection of Adonis closely resembles the story of the death and resurrection of Christ. This explains why a sixteenth-century Christian commentator, Hospinian, should have asserted that 'in allegory, St. George stands for Christ, the Dragon is the Devil, and the citizens of Silena are the human race redeemed by Christ'. It is clearly *this* interpretation of the story which induced the Church to give its

F

approval to a fable which, on the face of it, had the
closest possible relationship to such pagan dragon
stories as that of Perseus and Andromeda.

But now let us leave St. George for a bit and consider
some other kinds of dragon story. What about
treasure-guarding dragons? Typical of these was the
dragon Ladon who lay coiled around the tree which
bore the golden apples of immortal life in the Garden
of the Hesperides. Like St. George's dragon, Ladon
was sentimental as well as savage: he had as attendants
numerous beautiful maidens who, I fear, collaborated
with Hercules to bring about the dragon's downfall.
This dragon has a strong family resemblance to the
serpent in the Garden of Eden, but I leave you to work
that one out for yourselves.

And now royal ancestor dragons. I have already
mentioned Erichthonios, ancestor of kings of Athens.
Likewise the Emperors of China were descended from
dragons, and our own King Arthur too, though I am
not sure whether a Welshman would agree that Arthur's
father, Uthur Pendragon, was dragon in fact as well
as dragon in name. But anyway, I do assure you that
dragons often have kings as their descendants.

Now it seems rather a big jump from dragons as evil
monsters associated with the Devil to dragons as deified
grandfathers. Some explanation seems called for.

The Greeks would have explained their dragon
ancestors after this fashion: the life or soul of a man is
the marrow of his backbone; when he dies this marrow
congeals and becomes a snake—which is why you so
often see snakes hanging around cave tombs. The souls
of heroes and kings of course become very large snakes,
that is dragons, and are to be worshipped accordingly.
Chinese dragonology is much more metaphysical.

The sky is male and the earth is female. The sky fertilises the earth with rain and the womb of the earth bears crops. Metaphysically the rain is produced through the operations of dragons; ritually it is produced by religious ceremonials carried out by the Emperor in person. Chinese dragons are thus very closely associated with rain-making on the one hand and with the person of the Emperor on the other. The idea that the Emperor was descended from dragons served to fit the rain-making agricultural rites into the more general Chinese scheme that every man makes pious offerings to the shades of his ancestors.

In China proper, dragons—that is the creatures whom the Chinese call *lung*—were nearly always respected as emblems of the Emperor; they were never reckoned as evil monsters in the European style. This has led some scholars to maintain that the Chinese *lung* is, despite his appearance, really quite a distinct species from St. George's dragon. However, I have evidence to the contrary. Some years ago in the Kachin Hills on the borders of China and Burma I came across some indubitable Chinese dragons who possessed nearly all the usual European characteristics. They were called Numraw. In the first place, they were the ancestors of the local Kachin chief in just the same way as dragons were ancestors of the Chinese Emperors; indeed you might almost say that the Kachin chief was a dragon himself. It was quite polite to refer to the chief's palace as 'the cave of the dragon'. Then again, Numraw were treasure-guarding dragons; they watched over all sacred places and religious rituals and if anyone should make a mistake in the proceedings woe betide him. Incidentally these latter vengeful Numraw, like their Greek counterparts the Erinyes, were female. Then there were Numraw who were straightforward monsters; they lived down below in the valley and lay in wait for the Kachins whenever the latter were rash enough to go down the mountain to get across the river. These valley-dwelling monsters looked very like human beings to me; they were the Shans, traditional enemies of the Kachins. Once, long ago, the Shans had been their overlords.

And finally, I came across St. George himself—in this form:

'Once upon a time there was a princess who was betrothed to marry a prince, but the prince delayed the marriage and the princess had a child by another lover. Now this was a bad business, for it meant that the child would be treated as a slave by his adopted father, the prince. So the princess was very unhappy. One day she went down with her baby to the river to wash her hair. When she looked up the baby had disappeared, and all that could be seen were the tell-tale tracks of a dragon. So the princess prayed to the Thunder-Saint for help, and the Thunder-Saint took pity on her and struck the dragon's cave with his lightning so that the mountain was split open, the dragon was killed, and the baby returned to its mother.'

You will agree, I hope, that on the basis of such a story these Kachin Numraw can certainly be classed as dragons of an entirely orthodox variety.

What sort of explanation can we offer for the existence and popularity of dragon stories? I fancy that there are many different kinds of explanation and that all of them are partly true and partly false. If someone were to maintain, for example, that the Chinese dragon is derived from the image of a waterspout or whirlwind sweeping across the plains of

Northern China, I could not contradict him, but I myself find arguments of a psychological kind much more convincing. For example, a psycho-analyst would probably explain the contradictory nature of dragon character in this way: The hero-saint is always myself, the 'I'. The dragon, in contrast, is always my parent, whom I respect as an ancestor yet secretly hate as a rival. In killing the dragon I kill my parent.

Farfetched though this may seem, there is certainly something to it. Even in story-telling, killing dragons is never an end in itself, it is all mixed up with killing human beings. Œdipus, who killed his father by mistake, then killed a dragon, the Sphinx, on purpose. (However, the Sphinx was female; she committed suicide after Œdipus had guessed her riddle, the answer to which was, in effect, 'the infant child grows into a man'. Later in the story, when Œdipus has discovered that his wife Jocasta is also his mother, Jocasta commits suicide. The Sphinx thus seems to 'stand for' Jocasta and not for Laius, the father whom Œdipus had killed.) Perseus having killed two dragons on purpose, then killed his grandfather by mistake. St. George having killed the dragon, then dies a martyr—and just as a dragon has seven heads, St. George has seven deaths. In the Kachin story which I have just told the immediate sequel is that the Thunder-Saint sends an emissary to kill the chief, the princess's uncle, and so on.

Put crudely, we may say that there is always someone whom one would secretly like to get rid of—it may be a father, or an uncle, or a mother-in-law, or simply the boss, but, whoever it is, the fantasy of reducing the hated one to a dragon and then chopping his or her head off provides considerable private satisfaction.

But I think fantasies of this kind have political as well as personal significance. To return to the Kachins again. The story about the princess and the Thunder-Saint is part of a saga which is used to justify revolt against tyrannical chiefs. The dragon who is killed represents, quite certainly, the chief himself. And so too with the original St. George. Perhaps he is not very historical but, in legend at least, he *did* defy the tyrant Emperor. St. George was a revolutionary republican.

The difference between good dragons and bad dragons is simply a difference of political viewpoint. In China proper the Emperor was the father of his people and dragons were good dragons; on the fringes of territorial China the Emperor is remembered as a foreign tyrant and dragons are bad dragons. Stories about bad dragons are all definitely radical. Our own approval of St. George goes very well with the slogan 'Britons never, never shall be slaves', but I am always a bit surprised when I find such a thoroughgoing anarchist disguised as an Empire Crusader!

SUGGESTIONS FOR FURTHER READING

The story of St. George, the Princess and the Dragon derives mainly from the *Legenda Aurea*, an account of the lives of the saints written by Jacobus de Voragine, Archbishop of Genoa, about 1280. An English version was printed by Caxton in 1483. My version is a contraction of that given by S. Baring-Gould in *Curious Myths of the Middle Ages* (1884). Sir E. A Wallis Budge in *George of Lydda, the Patron Saint of England* (1930), provides a summary of nearly all the multifarious legends concerning St. George and traces their sources. (Scholars dispute as to the dating of the earliest extant inscriptions referring to Saint George. See Budge, pp. 16, 18, where various dates from A.D. 197 onwards are considered.) A simpler work for the general reader is G. J. Marcus *Saint George of England* (1929). The iconography of St. George is the subject of a number of monographs of which M. H. Bulley *St. George for Merrie England* (56 illustrations, 1908) is one.

Dragon stories in general have been studied by comparative folklorists from various points of view; among the most comprehensive of such studies are E. S. Hartland, *The Legend of Perseus* (3 vols., 1894) and K. Ranke, *Die Zwei Brüder* (Helsinki, 1934). For the dragon ancestry of Chinese emperors see M. Granet, *Chinese Civilisation* (1930). The seemingly paradoxical association of dragons (serpents) with beneficent power on the one hand and witchcraft on the other is a feature of a number of recent anthropological accounts, in particular see M. Wilson, *Good Company*, Chapter V (1951). The background for the Kachin dragons mentioned in this chapter is to be found in E. R. Leach, *Political Systems of Highland Burma* (1954).

IX

The Isles of the Bless'd

T. C. LETHBRIDGE

IN a poem called *Ulysses*, which thousands of schoolboys have learned by heart, Tennyson makes the hero say:

> It may be we shall touch the Happy Isles,
> And see the great Achilles, whom we knew.

What were these 'Happy Isles'? Is this story of the Isles of the Bless'd a myth or a legend? The subject is not quite so easy as some of those already discussed, and really falls into three distinct phases: there is the Greek side of it, the Celtic and the Norse.

Now the Greek side of the story starts as long ago as about 800 B.C. It is not mentioned in Homer's *Odyssey*. It comes up, first of all, in some poems, the works of a man called Hesiod. He wrote a series of poems containing various myths and stories. Among them was one that the gods rewarded certain people who were extremely outstanding and were considered worthy of it. They transported them west of the Pillars of Hercules, which, of course, are the Straits of Gibraltar, and settled them down on the Islands of the Bless'd, where they thoroughly enjoyed themselves indefinitely. They never died, they just lived in the Islands of the Bless'd in the utmost luxury.

And as far as the Greek side of it goes, that is practically all there is to the story. The question whether it is a myth or a legend now comes up. If it was a myth, it seems very odd that the Greeks should have invented it, because they were people with their main interests and outlook facing towards the East. Why should they pick on a place beyond the Pillars of Hercules, where, as far as we know, they had never been at that time? On the other hand there had been, from a very much earlier age, a continual traffic in shipping from Palestine and, perhaps, even from Egypt, westward through the Mediterranean, and out through the Pillars of Hercules to a place which is known in the Bible as Tarshish, but which was known to the classical world as Tartessos. Tartessos, or Tarshish, whichever we like to call it, was visited by the ships of King Solomon, and that dates, perhaps, a hundred years before this poem of Hesiod. Solomon's ships used to go there, spending three years in the round voyage. They returned to Palestine with, or more probably took from it, all kinds of things which we have heard of—ivory and apes and peacocks, so it is said. But as far as we know, no Greeks ever went through the Straits, or the 'Gut' as it used to be called in Nelson's day, until a man called Kolaios of Samos went there, much later, about 620 B.C.

It therefore rather looks as if this story about the Isles of the Bless'd, which the Greeks got hold of, was not their own invention, but was something which they had picked up from some other people. We cannot be definite about that, of course, or about any of these other tales, but it does look suspicious.

Now we must leave the Greeks, move across the world, jump through time, and go to Ireland in the

Dark Ages. Irish folklore is full of stories which are described as Celtic tales. They deal with a pleasant, happy, or bless'd land beyond the sunset.

The Celtic stories all treat of the same kind of country as that mentioned in the Greek tales. There is the Land of Youth, the Land of Women, the Plain of Pleasure, and so on. Just the same kind of things happen: men go for very long voyages across the sea; sometimes they are said to have gone in glass boats, but having seen the boats of the Polar Eskimo, I know quite well that a skin-boat when it has been well polished and nicely greased looks almost as clear as glass, and I find no difficulty in swallowing that side of the story. These men went for many weeks right across the Western Ocean, and they returned—if they ever did return—as very old men. The tales apparently grew out of their exploits.

These stories were in fact mostly written down many years later. The particular ones that are of most interest to us here are the stories of St. Brendan. They were written down in the eleventh century, and are not exactly travel tales but a kind of conglomeration of stories dealing with the sea. St. Brendan or Brandan is apparently an historical character. He was born in the west of Ireland about A.D. 484, and was educated by another saint, called St. Erc, in mathematics and astronomy, as well as Latin and Hebrew. He is said to have left his native Ireland in A.D. 545 and to have made two prodigious voyages in a western direction. The first one hardly concerns us, because he apparently went in a skin-boat round by way of Iceland and Greenland and Newfoundland. But on the second one, in which he went in a wooden ship with quite a number of companions, he sailed due west for forty days and arrived in a land of fogs and shoals. As far as one can judge from the accounts, there were walruses and seals there, with plenty of fish, and it seems almost beyond doubt that he landed up on the Grand Banks of Newfoundland. From there he went south and came to a land of hostile, dark savages. And eventually, after visiting a land where there was a single Irish monk, who was apparently a survivor of an earlier party, he returned to Ireland, and added his piece to this mass of talk about the happy land beyond the sunset.

I have no doubt myself that quite a lot of the statements in the stories of St. Brendan are true accounts of some real voyages, but mixed up with them are curious little bits of what you might call fable, which have been brought in from other sources. For instance, there is a story of how Brendan and his monks started to cook a meal on the back of a whale which they mistook for a sandbank; and this incident is found again in a story which we all know—Sinbad the Sailor in the *Arabian Nights*. Obviously there was some sort of general pool, as we might call it, of sailors' talk, and some of the stories from this general pool got into the life of St. Brendan. There is also, of course, a certain possibility that some of the tales in St. Brendan's life may have come from Norse seamen who, in the eleventh century when this life was written down, were making voyages not only to Iceland but to Greenland and apparently to America.

The Norse tales are recorded in sagas, and the sagas are really histories of important families in Norway or in Iceland or wherever else they happened to live. For instance, there might be innumerable voyages made all round the world by people who did not belong to important families, but they would never have been recorded in sagas at all. It so happens, however, that sagas have been recorded and written down which concern the life of Eric the Red, who was the first settler in Greenland, and of members of his family who also did rather remarkable feats. Eric the Red settled in Greenland somewhere at the end of the tenth century, and a man known as Leif the Lucky went over to visit him. The course of this voyage seems like a perfectly straightforward traveller's tale: he was blown past Cape Farewell, the south point of Greenland, and fetched up somewhere—we do not know where—on the coast of North America. From there, after spending a little time examining the place, he managed to work his way back to Eric the Red's home in Greenland. When he got there, he described what had happened to him; he apparently was not in the least bit interested in the discovery of America or anything to do with that. Eric, however, was rather annoyed that he had not taken more pains to find out what sort of land it was. As a result of all the talk that went on through the subsequent winter, when of course there is very little to do in Greenland because of the cold, other members of the same household decided to go and have a look at the land which Leif had discovered. Leif, incidentally, is called Leif the Lucky, not because he discovered America—which he did not think lucky at all—but because he picked a shipwrecked crew off a reef. That gave him his nickname.

The next part of the story centres round a man whose name was Thorfinn Karlsefni. He is the real explorer of North America. He went out there, some say with two ships, others say with three, actually determined to settle. The accounts that have been preserved of his voyage read extremely unostentatiously: they are exactly as if someone had come back and told a true account of adventure at a time when people were expecting something a little unusual, but nothing miraculous. For instance, there are accounts of how, when they got to America, they dug pits below high-water mark; when the tide came in and went out again they caught halibut in the pits—which is just the sort of thing that was done in the Hebrides up till about fifty years ago.

Anyhow, the expedition went across to America, and after a while owing to various dissensions, quarrels and other difficulties, it returned. The main story, as far as it goes, is absolutely straight; but mixed up in it are little bits of description which look as if they had been taken out of some of the earlier tales like that of St. Brendan. For instance, there is much talk of grapes growing wild, which gave the country its name of Vineland, of self-sown fields of wheat and other marvels, which sound very much as if they belonged to the older stories and not to the very prosaic expedition story of the Norsemen.

As far as the literary evidence goes, that is all that need be said. But I should like to point out that it is perfectly possible that sailors, especially traders of Tartessos, might have been blown across the North Atlantic and have reached America. The winds are right and, as a kind of half-way house, you have a very high mountain peak in the Azores, which can be seen from at least a hundred and fifty miles away. In the Azores, as far as one can gather from the reports at any rate, Carthaginian coins have actually been found. There does not seem to me to be any doubt that in classical times some people got as far as the Azores, and with the North-East Trades to blow them farther, there is no reason why, having got so far, they should not have gone on. Just enough has been found by archæologists to hint that there might be some possible connexion between the early cultures of the Mediterranean and those of North America, especially Central America. There are certain types of stone axes, certain female figurines and certain kinds of painted pottery which might suggest that at some time one or two, or perhaps three or four, ships' crews might have arrived on the far side, and instructed the peoples over there in the use of various things they knew at home.

We must now try to decide whether these stories are myth or legend. In other words, whether they are pure make-believe or whether they had some foundation in fact. As far as we can see, the Greek stories could have been make-believe, although it seems improbable that they are complete make-believe. It is more likely that they came from some sailors' tales from some other country. As time goes on, we get the Irish stories which look very much less like make-believe and more like distorted fact. Then, finally, we get the Norse voyages, and very little make-believe seems to come into them. And so the Isles of the Bless'd have shrunk, or grown, from some nebulous, unattainable, wonderful land beyond the sunset, to a thing we now know very well as the United States of America.

* * *

SUGGESTIONS FOR FURTHER READING

Under the heading of 'Elysium', the *Encyclopædia Britannica* gives full references to the main Greek sources for the story of the Isles of the Bless'd. Some of these are quoted and the Isles are described in Chapter IV of Professor H. J. Rose's *Handbook of Greek Mythology* (Revised ed., 1953). M. P. Nilsson in *A History of Greek Religion* (2nd ed., 1949) claims that the idea originated in pre-Hellenic Crete.

Probably the best recent book on Vinland is *The Norse Discoveries and Explorations in America* by Edward Reman (1949); he gives two versions of the Vinland sagas, but I cannot always agree with his conclusions. The Norse and Irish voyages are discussed in Chapters 7 and 8 of *Herdsmen and Hermits* by T. C. Lethbridge (1950).

Those who can read Latin will find the story of St. Brendan's voyage in *Acta Sancti Brendani*, edited by the Rt. Rev. P. F. Moran (Dublin, 1872). Some opinions on the voyages of St. Brendan will be found in *The Anglo-Norman Voyages of St. Brendon* edited by E. G. R. Waters (1928), and *Brendan the Navigator. An Interpretation* by George A. Little (Dublin, 1945).

18. Aerial view of Stonehenge from the north-east

X

The Druids
and Stonehenge

STUART PIGGOTT

OF course, Stonehenge is neither a myth nor a legend, nor are the Druids. Nothing could be more substantial than the enormous stones set up on Salisbury Plain; nobody more matter-of-fact (even to dullness) than Julius Cæsar, who is one of our main informants on the Druids. But legends have grown up about both, and if myth is defined as a story based on pure imagination, there has been considerable myth-making as well.

The legend of the Druids and Stonehenge is a learned one. It is not one of those whose origins are lost in a vague past of folk-tale, and so far as it has ever been really a popular belief, it has become so because of the adoption of out-of-date views current among scholars in the past, by people attracted to the ideas by their romantic appeal. What is so interesting about the legend, in fact, is that we can see pretty well how and when it began, and how it was built up and elaborated later: this is when the myths began.

The general form the story takes would, I suppose, be something like this. The Ancient Britons had a priesthood called the Druids; they were philosophers, poets and seers whose doctrines are known in detail and contain hints of Higher Things. They had an elaborate series of ceremonial observances and solemn ritual which took place in the open air, in circles of standing stones. Of these Druid temples, so the story goes, the greatest and most magnificent is Stonehenge, where particularly impressive ceremonies were performed at sunrise on Midsummer Day, when the rising sun first strikes the Altar Stone. Some part of the Druid doctrine has been passed down to, or rediscovered in, the present day, and the modern Midsummer Day ceremony at Stonehenge represents a very ancient tradition. There is an idea, too, that the Druids at Stonehenge are connected with those of the Welsh Eisteddfod, both being the modern representatives of an enlightened pre-Roman priesthood.

If I have given a fair idea of the current Druid legend (and I think I have, on the whole), it contains the most fascinating mixture of real fact, misunderstood fact, pure supposition and a reckless jumping to exciting conclusions. Let us examine it, bit by bit, and see what we can make of it. And first, the Druids themselves.

There is no doubt about the Druids having had a real existence all right, and about their being a pre-Roman, Celtic priesthood. What we know about them is derived from the incidental, and always tantalisingly brief, mentions of them by Greek and Roman writers from about 200 B.C. to A.D. 350 or 400, and from a very few inscriptions. The classical writers were not very interested in Druids, the priests of the barbarian Celts, unless they came up against them in the way of business, as Cæsar did in his Gaulish campaigns. On the whole, and quite reasonably, they wrote about them not as anthropologists or students of comparative religion, but rather as a colonial administrator sixty or seventy years ago might have recorded a few of the more startling facts about the witch-doctors and medicine men he had heard of or encountered in Africa or the Orient.

From this evidence, and by inference from what we know of other early religions, we can sketch an outline picture of the Druids around the time of Cæsar or later. The Celtic peoples of Gaul and Britain seem to have shared a similar social structure and some religious concepts with other speakers of the Indo-European languages: society was divided into three main groups, the priesthood, the warrior-aristocracy and the rest. You could be an aristocrat and a Druid, and during Cæsar's campaigns in Gaul it was only natural that the Druids should form the centre of the resistance movement. Although they had no writing, the Celtic peoples possessed a considerable literature transmitted by word of mouth, and Cæsar tells us that much of the novitiate's training for the priesthood was devoted to learning 'innumerable verses' by heart: this is just the same as the strict Brahmin tradition of the present day.

There is no escaping from the fact that an important feature of Druid ritual was human sacrifice. This was more than the Romans, usually so tolerant in religious observances, could stand for, and the deliberate policy of stamping out Druidism within the Empire is wholly understandable on this count alone. The other ritual of which we know something is the gathering of the mistletoe from the oak (on which it so rarely grows), followed by the sacrifice of two white bulls. Of Druid doctrines we know little, except that they

believed in some form of immortality and in trans-
migration of souls: the Celtic belief in an after-life
was so strong, indeed, that they would lend money on
an IOU to be repaid in the other world! But by and
large, there is nothing about the Druids or their religion
which distinguishes them from other contemporary
barbarian communities on the fringes of the classical
world. But it should be said that no classical writer
talks about Druid temples, except those which were
mere clearings in the forest.

Druidism as a cult must have been exterminated
during the Roman occupation of Britain, but something presumably lingered on in Ireland and perhaps
elsewhere into Early Christian times. The Welsh
Eisteddfod was a medieval institution (the first we know
of was in 1176) in which poets, singers and musicians
assembled, and the introduction of Druid ceremonies
of the present kind seems to have been in 1791 on
Primrose Hill. They first appeared in an Eisteddfod
in 1819, in the garden of a Carmarthen pub. But
more of this later.

Now for Stonehenge. I will not disguise the fact
that Stonehenge is a pretty puzzling monument, but
we have got somewhere in understanding it. I would
remind you that it is a circular structure of simple, but
by no means unaccomplished, architectural qualities.
An outer peristyle, or circle of uprights with a con-
tinuous ring of lintels, encloses five huge trilithons, or
three-stone structures each of two uprights and a
lintel, set like five symbolic gateways on a horseshoe
plan. Inside the outer peristyle the planning, but not
the upright and lintel systems, is repeated in smaller
stones set in a circle and in a horseshoe. The bigger
stones, making up the main structure, come from north

Wiltshire some 25 miles away and are sarsens; the smaller are a mixture of igneous rocks from Pembrokeshire. The whole of these stone structures lie within a bank and a ditch set a long way out from it. There is a ceremonial approach leading to the monument, bounded by a pair of flanking banks and ditches, and in the course of this, near the entrance through the bank and ditch, is a single upright stone known as the Heel Stone. And this entrance and ceremonial approach point towards the Midsummer sunrise (Plate 1, *the frontispiece*, and Plate 18, facing p. 96).

There are other features and complications of course, but we have not time to go into those now. Excavation has shown that Stonehenge is complex, built and altered over some centuries of time, just as almost any English cathedral. The bank and ditch is part of the earliest monument, dating from round about 1700 to 1600 B.C. The stones (themselves representing more than one phase of construction) date from a century or two later. The date for the beginning of Stonehenge is supported by a radio-carbon reading as well as archæological evidence; the date of the reconstruction receives new support from the recognition this summer of carvings of Bronze Age tools and weapons of specific types on some of the stones.

So Stonehenge is a monument of the middle of the second millennium B.C. But the Druids are the priesthood of the Celtic peoples a little around and before the beginning of the Christian era. No ancient tradition associates the two. How then did they come to be brought together in popular legend?

One of the most engaging characters of the later seventeenth century was John Aubrey, country gentleman, gossip, biographer and antiquary, Fellow of the

Royal Society—'an ingeniose Gent' in the phrase of his day. He discovered the great circle at Avebury and planned it; collected more details in the field and the study, and drafted a book on British field archæology of which the main part dealt with stone circles such as Avebury, Stonehenge, Long Meg and so on. No idea of a prehistoric time-scale existed then, of course—to make things pre-Roman was daring enough. Aubrey's classical education supplied the Druids as a pre-Roman priesthood, and his field-work had revealed ceremonial structures of prehistoric date. He first put it forward—but only as a tentative suggestion—that the circles might be Druid temples.

But others were less cautious. William Stukeley too was an antiquarian field-worker, inspired by Aubrey's unpublished notes to carry on at Avebury, and to do more at Stonehenge, in the 1720's. But he enjoyed speculating beyond the bounds of his evidence, and as time went on theories took the place of facts, and the Druids had their propagandist. By the time of his death in 1765 the idea that Stonehenge and other Bronze Age stone circles were Druid temples had been enthusiastically adopted not only by antiquarians but by the intelligent public at large. Romanticism was in the air. Macpherson's *Ossian* concoctions, Gray's Bardic poems, and those of Collins and Mason, even Blake's prophetic poems, are not only in the full spirit of the times, but at times explicitly develop the Druid myth—for surely it is a myth by now, this noble and enlightened band of ancient philosophers. The Ancient Order of Druids, the origin of the modern Benefit Society, was founded in 1781 as a more mysterious and less beneficial institution, and as we have seen, the Welshman Iolo Morganwg had the bright idea of adding Druids to the Eisteddfod (and incidentally forging the documents to support his case).

The Druid story endeared itself to the popular mind and, as is always the case, general knowledge inevitably lags behind development in the fields of scholarship, and perpetuates views long ago discarded by those best qualified to judge. It must be admitted, too, that the Druids are, in their legendary form, most satisfactorily picturesque. It is hard doctrine for the non-archæologist to accept that we do not know what sort of religion lay behind the building of Stonehenge, nor what ceremonies were performed there; it is harder, too, when you add that such things just cannot be discovered by archæological means, however much techniques may be refined and elaborated, but only by the medium of the historical documents which in the nature of things are non-existent for the period and monuments in question. One can hardly wonder at people turning from this rather bleak prospect, and preferring to think in terms of Druids and Bards and Ovates proclaiming noble (if vague) doctrines of high import and prehistoric ancestry at Stonehenge on Midsummer morning, or at the Eisteddfod wearing robes of office designed by the Victorian artist Hubert von Herkomer.

What has happened is, as I said earlier on, an intriguing mixture of fact and fantasy. Druids and Stonehenge are real enough aspects of archæology; Celtic religion and ceremonial sites of the second millennium B.C. are both rewarding subjects for study, but no connexion between the two can be shown to have existed. Stonehenge was already an Ancient Monument by the time we first hear of Druids. And the Druids, in the form in which the public knows them to-day, are a picturesque invention of the Romantic Movement. If any bold spirit among them were to try to make a return to primitive doctrine and ritual as recorded in our only authorities, the classical writers, the results would certainly be front-page news, but their performance would be as rapidly and forcibly curbed as in the days of the Roman Empire.

SUGGESTIONS FOR FURTHER READING

T. D. Kendrick's *The Druids* (2nd ed. 1928) is still by far the best book on the subject, though of course out of date archæologically. The development of the Druid myth is dealt with here and in Stuart Piggott, *William Stukeley: An Eighteenth Century Antiquary* (1950), and the Eisteddfod connexion is discussed by Iorwerth Peate, 'The Gorsedd of the Bards of Britain', *Antiquity*, xxv (1951), pp. 13–15.

There is no up-to-date book on Stonehenge, and the recent work there is altering conclusions reached at an earlier stage. Knowledge to 1949 is summarised by Stuart Piggott, 'Stonehenge Reviewed', in *Aspects of Archæology* (1951), pp. 274–92, and the most complete treatment of the site will be that in the forthcoming *Victoria County History of Wiltshire*, Vol. I, by Stuart Piggott and C. F. C. Hawkes.

XI

The 'Lost Continent' of Atlantis

JOHN BRADFORD

PEOPLE in every age are credulous in their own way. Just now it is outer space, and weird objects in the sky, that are common topics of speculation. But the idea of lost lands, cities and peoples has always had a strong fascination, and the life of Colonel Fawcett was an extreme instance of its overmastering power. From devoted research to fanaticism, however, can be a short and easy step. In the wider field of popular thought, the taller the story, and the more inaccessible its setting, the more compelling it usually is, and the greater its capacity for survival in spite of disproof.

More of us, I suspect, have read Conan Doyle's tale, *The Maracott Deep*, about an imaginary search for Atlantis under the sea, than have read the first written description of the place by the Greek philosopher Plato, composed just before 350 B.C. But we must start with Plato's account, so as to understand the later embroideries on it. Even so, and if we take him literally, the story only comes to us at third or fourth hand. But there is good reason to believe that he intended it as a parable.

Plato naturally gives the tale a respectable parentage, but sets it well back in the past. He said it was told some sixty years before, at the house of Socrates in Athens, by a certain Critias who claimed that it had been handed down in his family from Solon the Wise, one hundred and fifty years earlier still.

For what it's worth, here is the story. Solon visited the priests of the temple at Sais in Egypt. Like learned antiquarians, they exchanged stories of the past. The priests told Solon that the Greeks had still a lot to learn about their own history, and they trumped his efforts by a spectacular tale which had the added merit of glorifying Athens as the saviour of the world. Nine thousand years ago, said the priests, there was a powerful island-state outside the Pillars of Hercules (the Straits of Gibraltar, as we say to-day), on the edge of the Ocean—an ordinary classical figure of speech for 'dim distance'. This island, they said, was larger than Libya and Asia (the modern North Africa and Middle East), and other islands were reached from it. Its armies invaded the Atlantic coasts of Europe and Africa, but Athens, though deserted by her allies, finally defeated them. Afterwards, however, there were violent earthquakes and floods, and in a single terrible day and night the island of Atlantis sank beneath the waves. Thick mud still made the sea impassable there (Fig. iv).

In the second part of Plato's account imagination is given fuller play. In the middle of the chief island lay a fertile plain ringed by mountains. There were palaces, temples, bridges and ships. Buildings were adorned with silver, gold and ivory. To add to the excitement, there was a mysterious, precious substance called 'orichalcum' on which the laws were written.

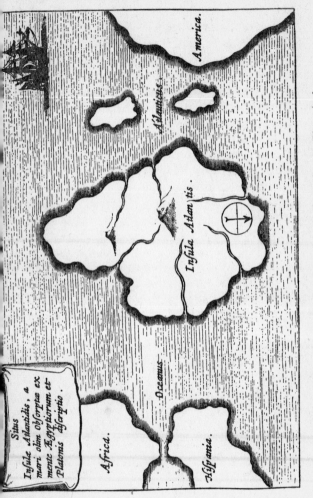

Fig. iv. The island of Atlantis, based on the description by Plato, is shown in *Mundus Subterraneus*, by Athanasius Kircher (1644).

North is at the bottom of the map, which is best inspected upside down.

Everything was efficiently planned. Absolute power was vested in ten kings, and there was a huge army of javelin men and charioteers. But these people, descended from gods, and once virtuous and happy, became degenerate, and the mighty god Zeus decided to punish them.

Plato left the story unfinished, but he had made his point. The disaster to Atlantis showed how a luxurious 'Great Power' could be defeated by a small, virtuous Greek state; with moral conclusions that would be obvious to his contemporaries. There is no doubt that Plato intended to be believed, but there is every doubt about the tale coming from Solon. The best authorities, like Jowett, are all agreed that Plato created it deliberately to play its part in the context of the great themes he was unfolding in the *Dialogues*. But did he possibly redecorate some old folk-tale?

I am going to distinguish two aspects of the question, first dealing with the picture of life in Atlantis and then saying something of where it is alleged to have been. Plato deliberately made life in Atlantis recognisable to his contemporaries, just as medieval painters clothed biblical figures in the dress of their own contemporary fashion. The details of the number of chariots, temples, and so forth would have seemed reasonable to the Greeks' notion of the past. But though they were nearer in time to prehistory, we to-day have a much wider knowledge of prehistory than they. And the more Plato piles on the details to convince, the more certainly do we know to-day that they were created for effect. The sort of life in Atlantis that Plato described was a complete impossibility, either at the suggested date of about 10,000 B.C. or for many thousands of years afterwards. All archæologists agree that at this time Southern Europe and North Africa were in a Mesolithic, 'Middle Stone Age', culture, peopled by primitive nomadic hunters and fishers using simple stone tools, which have been found in great quantities. Cities, canals and golden statues were as far beyond their technical abilities as they are beyond those of an aboriginal tribesman in Australia to-day.   The life depicted in Atlantis is complete myth and fiction.   So, if you think of deep-sea trawling off north-west Africa, you may land a *Chascanopsetta lugubris*, a rare and sad-looking fish, but there will be no gold statues!

In later times the Atlantis story did not develop much, until the discovery of America set curious tongues wagging again.   In 1675, a Swede named Rudbeck claimed that Atlantis had been in Sweden, and since then it has been traced to many countries, including a kingdom of Mu in Central America and a lost land off the coast of Tunisia; it has even been linked with the destruction of the Palace of Minos at Knossos in Crete about 1450 B.C.

In Victorian days, when the idea of the spread of human races and inventions from a single source was so popular, there was a small boom in speculations about the Atlantis story.   The most remarkable book was *Atlantis: the Antediluvian World*, by Ignatius Donnelly, a member of the United States Congress. He followed this up with a still stranger work entitled *Ragnarok, or The Age of Fire and Gravel*, which claimed that a comet hit the earth in the remote past and had caused most of its land and sea masses; and then he capped this with *The Great Cryptogram, or Francis Bacon's Cipher in the so-called Shakespeare Plays*.   That will give you an idea of his interests.

His book on Atlantis was a hotch-potch collection of facts and fancies from all over the world, for he believed that the destruction of Atlantis was part of a world-wide catastrophe, and lavish parallels were drawn between ancient peoples on both sides of the Atlantic. All the 'old faithfuls' of antiquarianism were trotted out: stone circles, pyramids, mummification and sun-worship—all to be spread eastwards and westwards by refugees from Atlantis. Alas for such misplaced ingenuity! It is a dangerous delusion that prehistory can be easily unravelled by anyone, and requires no technical training. Imagine, as a comparison, what would happen if you asked a lawyer to assemble an atomic cyclotron. He would probably emerge with something resembling a giant coffee-grinder, and plenty of parts left over! In passing, I may also mention a serious book,[1] dating from 1909, which set out to give a full account of daily life in Atlantis as obtained by clairvoyance, a superphysical effort of memory. According to this, the upper classes in Atlantis, like Victorian 'carriage folk', had their private conveyances, but these were air-ships!

Phantastical details were liberally piled on. In shape these air-ships 'were boat-like, but they were invariably decked over, for when at full speed it could not have been convenient, even if safe, for any on board to remain on the upper deck. Their propelling and steering gear could be brought into use at either end. But the all-interesting question is that relating to the power by which they were propelled. In the earlier times it seems to have been personal "vril" that supplied the motive-power—whether used in conjunction with any mechanical contrivance matters not much. . . .' 'The maximum speed attained was about 100 m.p.h., the course of flight never being a straight line but always in the form of long waves, now approaching and now receding from the earth. . . . Hills of about 1,000 feet were the highest they could cross.' In warfare the air-ships tried to turn each other upside down, but luckily there were 'tubes' by which the unfortunate things could be righted. A detailed and enjoyable description is given of an air-boat in which, on one occasion, three ambassadors from a king in northern Poseidonis (Atlantis) went to call on the southern court. We are told, too, of the epic struggle between the 'white emperors' who observed the Good Law and the 'black emperors' who followed Sorcery, and that 'the rude simplicity of Stonehenge was in-tended as a protest against the extravagant ornament and over-decoration of the existing temples in Atlantis'. In their later days they possessed co-education, poison gas and a coinage engraved with the triple mountain visible from the southern capital. A set of four coloured maps is added, showing 'Atlantis at its Prime' and 'Atlantis in its Decadence', and gives a global picture from one million years ago to 9564 B.C. ('final sub-mergence'). The detailed events recounted from this world of Cloud-Cuckoo-Land were supposed to have a moral or didactic significance—to show how the 'Masters of Wisdom' would guide mankind on the 'Path'. The whole fabrication is certainly instructive in other ways than those intended, and naturally I have quoted these extracts for entertainment purposes only! The moral of this story is that in Plato's time archæology did not exist to say him nay—but it is now our safeguard against distortions of history and race relations.

Now I shall turn to the second point: is there a possible geographical location for Atlantis? When we consider the existence of islands and coastlands that are now below sea-level, we are dealing with problems which have rational and straightforward explanations. In remote geological ages long before man, and continuing to the present day, the level of dry land relative to the sea has undergone a whole series of drastic changes in every part of the world. Therefore it is not surprising that almost all peoples (even the Eskimos) possess a number of epics or legends of floods. It is pointless to try to link them all together as a memory of a world catastrophe, as they have entirely different dates and causes. Some have even tried to link the destruction of Atlantis with the flood-story in the Bible, but we now know that the biblical flood was a relatively local affair. The Hebrew legend was based on a true story that was recast later. It originated in an historical event in Mesopotamia, and in the soil of Ur one can see the silt from the Euphrates piled high above the ruins of the pre-flood town (see Chapter IV). And all this, of course, was thousands of years after the supposed date of Atlantis.

Those who try to take the Atlantis story literally have pointed out that volcanic eruptions have wrecked many small islands in the past, and that there is plenty of evidence of eruptions from countries bordering the Atlantic, including the Canary Islands off north-west Africa. The islands of the Azores, in mid-Atlantic, seem their present favourite location for Atlantis, but even they admit that a volcanic eruption could not destroy a big island-continent. Curiosity is easily aroused about those little-known islands. To get a clearer personal picture of them, I examined the airphotographs of an aerial survey. Craters abound, but the soil is fertile. Colonised c. A.D. 1445, the Azores now have a quarter of a million inhabitants in a total area of 880 square miles. We may note in passing the uncertainty that surrounds the Carthaginian coins (third century B.C.) allegedly found as a hoard in a clay pot on Corvo island (the most westerly of the Azores) in 1749. The coins were published in 1778, but a modern attempt to trace them was unsuccessful.[2]

Small islands can, and do, still appear and disappear in the Central Pacific, through volcanic action, but these are only small losses of land here and there. In these archipelagoes there has been claimed a kind of rival to Atlantis, called Lemuria; and there are grounds for the belief that, early in the far-distant period known to geologists as the Tertiary, a large area of slightly elevated land in the Central Pacific did become covered by ocean, partly by subsidence and partly by an actual rise of sea-level. But this happened long, long before Man appeared.

Similarly, in the Atlantic, the Azores islands, which are the peaks of a broad submarine ridge that runs down the centre of the Atlantic floor, may be the visible remains of a land area which foundered about the end of the Mesozoic period. But this also would be long before Man. We can safely leave to the refutation of astronomers a fanciful 'Luna' theory that only about 15,000 years ago the earth captured the moon as its satellite, and that the latter's gravitational pull then piled up quantities of water in our lower latitudes, keeping much land submerged.

It comes to this then: Atlantis as an island-continent, within human history, is make-believe, and has to go. What are we left with? Primitive people often magnify a local disaster to huge proportions in their legends, for to them it affects their whole world.

H

And human prehistory is full of evidence of verifiable
changes in land and sea-levels, due to established
natural causes.

For example, there are many scientific proofs that
after the end of the last Ice Age the sea-level in western
Europe was rising gradually, as the ice-caps melted
and receded. In this period, between 10,000 and
5000 B.C., the Straits of Dover were opened, and salt
water from the expanding North Sea also flowed into
the Baltic, and changed it from a lake into a sea. And
there is the final breaching of the Straits of Gibraltar.
Frequently we find the stone implements of the contemporary Mesolithic hunters and fishers below the
modern tide-mark, in association with traces of submerged forests. This does not mean that the people
were drowned, but that the sea eventually covered
these camp sites on the shores.

Of course, the tendency of the sea to encroach on
the land continued to be important to a much later
date. For example, the maximum sea-level in the
Cambridge fens was not reached until about the year
'nought' B.C.–A.D. All this gives a respectable background of fact to the legends of Lyonesse—the submerged land off the Cornish coast—and even perhaps
to the lost town of 'Ys' off Brittany, and to the 'Isle
Verte' and 'Asmaide' (Mayda) which figure in folk-tales
from Gibraltar to the Hebrides. A hundred years ago
the latter islets were still marked on English charts[3]
north and north-east of the Azores. But none of these
has any direct connexion with the Atlantis story.

This continual nibbling at the coast might, here and
there, produce a sudden local inundation during
storms, but that can happen to-day—and there is no
need to invoke Atlantean catastrophes.

There was, in fact, not *one* such submergence in prehistory, but hundreds; not one Atlantis, but lots of small Atlantises; and it is hopeless to try to identify this yarn with any particular one of them. There is no longer need for any special concern about Atlantis, in its antique 'stage property' form. There are some questions, such as whether the earth is flat or round, about which we need be no longer troubled. If you want a real marine drama in human prehistory, it is best to keep to a real event like the opening of the Straits of Dover—that is, if you do not mind a drama with a thousand years or so between the acts!

NOTES

1. See *The story of Atlantis: A geographical, historical and ethnographical sketch*, by W. Scott-Elliot, 2nd ed. 1909.

2. See D. B. Harden, in *Antiquity*, 1948, p. 141.

3. See Norie's chart (with corrections to 1836). The islets were no longer shown on the 1861 chart by Charles Wilson.

XII

Nemi and
the Golden Bough

H. J. ROSE

FROM the seventh book of Vergil's *Æneid* we
learn that among the Italian chieftains who
came to do battle with Æneas was a certain Virbius,
son of Hippolytus and Aricia. He was reared, says
the poet, 'in Egeria's groves, around the watery shore
where stands the rich altar of Diana, her mercy-seat.
For rumour has it that after Hippolytus had fallen
to the wiles of his stepdame and, torn in pieces by his
terrified horses, had satisfied his father's vengeance
with his blood, he came back to the stars of heaven
and the airs that blow above us in the sky, being
recalled by Pæonian simples and by Diana's love. . . .
The kind Goddess of the Crossroads hid him in her
secret abode and left him to the care of Egeria the
nymph and to her woods, to live alone and lost to
fame in Italian forests, and to change his name to
Virbius. Hence also horny-hooved steeds are debarred
from the precincts of Her of the Crossroads and her
consecrated groves, because, scared by monsters of
the sea, they flung the car and its young driver headlong
upon the shore'.

A strange tale. Is it myth or legend? Why,

neither; it is a pseudo-myth. The sacred grove of
Diana—who to Vergil was the same as Artemis, a
Greek goddess who really does in some ways resemble
her—had no myth of its own, and someone supplied
the lack. He began from a terribly bad etymology.
Along with Diana in that sacred grove (*nemus*), which
gives its name to the modern village of Nemi, two
minor powers were worshipped. One was Egeria,
an obscure but old goddess who had another cult
just outside Rome; the other was a godling we know
almost nothing about except that his name was Virbius,
whatever that may mean. Our enterprising forger
of myths assumed that it meant *uir bis*, and casting
about to find someone who had been 'twice a man',
hit upon the ill-fated Hippolytus, son of the great
Athenian hero Theseus. Theseus' second consort,
the Cretan princess Phaidra, played Potiphar's wife to
Hippolytus' Joseph, and when Hippolytus repulsed
her she falsely accused him to her husband. Theseus
believed his wife and cursed his son. His own father,
the sea-god Poseidon, made the curse effective and
sent a sea-monster to frighten Hippolytus' horses as he
drove away from his father's house. They bolted,
and he was thrown from his chariot and dragged to
death. That, so far, is the tale told by Euripides in his
Hippolytus, and after him by Racine in his *Phèdre*. But
there was a variant: that Artemis, who loved Hippolytus for his zeal in hunting and for his chastity, persuaded
Asklepios the great physician to revive him, whereat
Asklepios was thunder-smitten by Zeus for upsetting
the natural order of things according to which when
a man dies he does not come back to life. A tale which
caught the imagination of two poets so excellent as
Vergil and Browning is evidently not to be despised,

but it left the way open for conjectures as to what became of Hippolytus after that. Italian inquirers found ready to hand the venerable grove of Diana, whom, as I have said, they identified with Artemis; they found Virbius worshipped there; they knew or could easily learn that there was a tabu on horses; and so it was not hard to construct their imitation myth. But they made no use at all of far stranger facts concerning Nemi (Plate 19, facing p. 97), and its ancient cult.

Now let us turn from Vergil to that great scholar whose centenary we are celebrating, the late Sir James Frazer. At the very beginning of his best-known work, *The Golden Bough*, after a description of Nemi and its remains, we read:

In the sacred grove there grew a certain tree round which at any time of the day, and probably far into the night, a grim figure might be seen to prowl. In his hand he carried a drawn sword, and he kept peering warily about him as if at every instant he expected to be set upon by an enemy. He was a priest and a murderer; and the man for whom he looked was sooner or later to murder him and hold the priesthood in his stead. Such was the rule of the sanctuary. A candidate for the priesthood could only succeed to office by slaying the priest, and having slain him, he retained office till he was himself slain by a stronger or a craftier.

Now this is no myth and no legend, genuine or artificial. It is plain fact, taken from the sober geographer Strabo, who was not romancing but setting down what he knew about Italy and the rest of the world. The 'priest who slew the slayer and shall himself be slain' was as real as any of the secular magistrates of the day and he bore a magisterial title.

It seems he was not called priest of Diana, but King of
the Grove, *rex nemorensis*. What can be the origin
of this strange dignity, to which clearly no one but a
desperate man would aspire?

Frazer devoted his immense learning to connecting
it with a religious phenomenon to which he, more than
anyone else, drew public attention. In considerable
parts of the world there exist, or have existed, kings
who were not only secular rulers, if indeed they were
that at all, and not only priests, but incarnate gods.
Since a god must obviously manifest himself in a healthy
and vigorous body, these incarnations have regularly
had a limit set to their mortal lives, and usually they
have either been put ceremonially to death after a
period of power and veneration, short or long, or else
at intervals they had to fight for their position, somewhat as the King of the Grove did for his. Now if
such divine kings existed in ancient Italy at a prehistoric date, we could easily conceive of the priest at
Nemi being a survival of them. For conservatism is so
characteristic of religious ritual everywhere that the
form may be preserved even when the original meaning
of the rite has been quite forgotten. The weak point
of the explanation is the extremely unsatisfactory
nature of the evidence adduced by Frazer to show that
any such kings ever existed in the classical world,
Greek or Italian. But there is this much truth in it,
that ancient Italian kings had some priestly functions,
as their Greek colleagues had, so that when kingship
was abolished, in both Rome and Athens, there yet
remained a magistrate who bore the title and carried
out the sacral obligations of a king. Indeed in Rome
he had no other functions, and kept his position for
life.

Now sacred groves are somewhat uncanny places, not least so to the ancient Mediterranean peoples. They seem to have been rather awed by their shade, for they loved the sunshine of their bright skies. Long after it had been forgotten why there was a King of the Grove who had to win his place by manslaying, human sacrifice was a feature of the ritual of German sacred forests, as we know from Tacitus. The victim of such a sacrifice need not be a person of high character; it is enough that he be in a state of ritual purity. A criminal will do, given the necessary formalities to bring him into this holy state. But the King of the Grove was a criminal, and doubly so; for he had not only slain Diana's priest, but violated her grove as well. There was, says the unknown commentator on Vergil whom we call Servius, a certain tree in that grove from which no one might break a branch; but if anyone chose to do so, that was his challenge to the King of the Grove, and the combat would then take place. If the challenger won, he had killed a man who deserved to die, and at the same time a holy man, the more acceptable perhaps to the goddess, who plainly had something grim about her. He might now enjoy this last remnant of a priestly kingship, till he in his turn became the victim.

But what was the tree, and why should its branches in particular be sacred, instead of the whole grove? 'Servius' is of opinion, and supports it with yet another artificial myth, that it was identical with the Golden Bough. In the sixth book of the *Æneid*, the hero is about to venture into the world of the dead to ask advice of the beatified spirit of his father Anchises. The Sibyl whom he consults tells him that he must have a passport of a strange kind.

On a dark tree there lurks a branch, golden-leaved and with pliant twigs of gold, consecrated as holy unto the Juno of the lower world. All the wood hides it, and the shadows of the dark valleys enclose it. . . . When thou hast duly found it, pluck it with thine hand, for it will readily and of its own will follow, if fate calls for thee, but if not, thou canst not overcome it by any strength nor tear it loose with hard iron.

Æneas goes in search of the bough, is guided to the right spot by the doves which are sacred to his divine mother Venus, and plucks it. Its appearance is like that of mistletoe, says the poet, but it is not mistletoe, it is gold. Thus provided, he gains admission to the mysterious under-world, sees its wonders and terrors, and meets and is counselled by his father.

That is enough for him and for his poet, but it still leaves a modern curious to know what this strange bough was. Once more, Frazer applies his gigantic erudition. Very briefly, and shorn of its many ramifications and side-issues, his explanation is that Vergil spoke truer than he perhaps knew concerning the Golden Bough, for originally at least it was mistletoe. That familiar parasite, as we know, or at all events as anyone who has read Frazer knows, is the object of many beliefs and customs. One thing it can be is someone's bundle of life, or external soul, the repository which contains his vital principle and so makes it impossible to kill him by wounding his body. If the Golden Bough really was mistletoe, if it was what the claimant plucked from the tree in Diana's grove, and if it contained, for any reason, the life or soul of the King of the Grove then in office, it is easy to see why it and not any casual bough from any tree was to be plucked by the challenger. It amounted to telling the King that his time had come, that his life was literally in another's hand, and that the newcomer stood ready to prove it. This much we may admit without accepting the rest of the theory concerning the origin of the whole weird business. But even so, it is clear that it is a hazardous structure, one 'if' piled upon another, a series of assumptions none of which is provably untrue, but none of which also can be demonstrated for Nemi or for the cult of Diana anywhere. Incidentally, mistletoe does not look like gold when it is growing, though if it is gathered and kept for some time it takes on a sort of golden colour.

But whether mistletoe grew in Diana's grove at Nemi or not, whether it was that or an ordinary branch of the sacred tree which the aspirant to the kingly priesthood gathered, the fact remains that there was in Vergil's day this strange and picturesque belief that somewhere and sometime there grew a wonderful branch, revealing itself as divine because it was of gold and not of growing wood with leaves on it, which would let itself be plucked only by one destined to some high exploit. The Vergilian passage gives us a welcome glimpse into a world of which we know very little, the beliefs current in ancient Italy, of which probably but a small fraction made their way into the literature which has come down to us. These beliefs seem to have been already dead in late antiquity, to judge by the strange speculations, half philosophic and half mythological, in which 'Servius' indulges when he tries to explain Vergil. Where 'Servius' failed, it is very doubtful if the much more learned Frazer, coming about a millennium and a half later, succeeded. But that most honest scholar never took his own theories very seriously; his interest was rather in the fascinating array of facts which he was able to gather. Whither they in turn led him he himself tells us in the preface to the final edition of his great work.

'In attempting to settle one question', he wrote, 'I had raised many more . . . and thus step by step I was lured on into far-spreading fields of primitive thought which had been but little explored by my predecessors. . . . Should my whole theory of this particular priesthood collapse—and I fully acknowledge the slenderness of the foundations on which it rests—its fall would hardly shake my general conclusions as to the evolution of primitive religion and society, which are founded on large collections of entirely independent and well-authenticated facts.'

So, not for the first time, fiction has led us to fact, and fact to wide general conclusions concerning man, his ways of life and his beliefs. These in turn deserve and have received critical scrutiny; Frazer's conclusions and his methods alike have been closely examined and in part rejected by later researchers. But the mass of authenticated facts remains, and no one who examines them aright can well fail to make his way to some clearer and truer ideas than he had before regarding the intellectual, social and religious history of his kind.

SUGGESTIONS FOR FURTHER READING

The great storehouse of facts and theories about Nemi, the Golden Bough, mistletoe, divine kings and much else is of course the third edition (1911–38) of Sir J. G. Frazer's best-known treatise, *The Golden Bough*. But for those who find its thirteen volumes (counting *Aftermath*) too much, there is his own epitome in one volume, from the same publishers. I have sketched a few of the beliefs and practices of the ancient Italians, especially the Romans, in *Primitive Culture in Italy* (1926; out of print, but not very hard to find second-hand) and *Ancient Roman Religion* (1949). There is much more in the works of the late W. Warde Fowler, especially *Roman Festivals of the Republic* (1908) and *Religious Experience of the Roman People* (1911). There is a good sketch of ancient beliefs and practices, with references to fuller treatments, in (Sir) W. R. Halliday's *Greek and Roman Folklore* (1927). I have dealt briefly with pseudo-myths in Chapter XI of my *Handbook of Greek Mythology* (5th ed., revised, 1953).

For Vergil, the best-known English rendering in verse is still that of Dryden. The Loeb edition (H. R. Fairclough, two vols.) contains a prose translation, and there is another and well-known one by the late J. W. Mackail (*Æneid*, 2nd ed., 1908; *Bucolics and Georgics*, 1889, now out of print).

a superb modern dictionary
of very convenient size

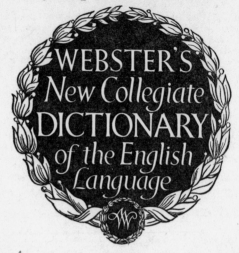

WEBSTER'S
New Collegiate
DICTIONARY
of the English
Language

[A GENUINE MERRIAM-WEBSTER DICTIONARY]

The *New Collegiate* is an entirely new post-war edition of the famous Collegiate Dictionary, revised and reset from cover to cover. It is based on the great *Webster's New International* to provide a handy-size dictionary, of the same high standard of scholarship, for students and the general reader. The definitions are those of the *New International* modified to obtain greater brevity and directness. Wherever they are needed phrases and sentences have been given to illustrate the meanings.

The entries concerned with the vocabularies of specialized subjects, from Accountancy to Zoology, benefit from the remarkable accuracy and completeness of the *New International* in the preparation of which over 200 specialist authorities have been employed as editors.

Over 125,000 entries · 2,300 illustrations · 1,230 pages · Buckram Binding specially reinforced · Sprinkled edges · 7⅛ × 10 × 1¾ inches (17·5 × 25 × 3·7 cm.) · Pronunciation of every entry · Synonyms · Full etymologies Biographical Dictionary · World Gazetteer.

★ ASK TO SEE IT AT ANY BOOKSHOP ★

This edition may not be supplied to the U.S.A. and its Dependencies, Canada, Newfoundland, Australasia.